THE NATIONS OF THE OLD TESTAMENT:

THEIR RELATIONSHIP WITH ISRAEL AND BIBLE PROPHECY

COMPILED BY HAYES PRESS

Copyright © Hayes Press 2017

All rights reserved. No part of this book may be reproduced, stored in a retrieval system, or transmitted in any form, without the written permission of Hayes Press.

Published by:

HAYES PRESS Publisher, Resources & Media,

The Barn, Flaxlands

Royal Wootton Bassett

Swindon, SN4 8DY

United Kingdom

www.hayespress.org

Unless otherwise indicated, all Scripture quotations are from The ESV® Bible (The Holy Bible, English Standard Version®), copyright © 2001 by Crossway, a publishing ministry of Good News Publishers. Used by permission. All rights reserved. Quotations marked RV or RV margin are from the Revised Version Bible (1885, Public Domain).

Table of Contents

CHAPTER ONE: THE PHOENICIANS (GEORGE PRASHER) 1

CHAPTER TWO: THE AMMONITES (C. MCKAY) 9

CHAPTER THREE: THE MOABITES (JACK MCILVENNA) 15

CHAPTER FOUR: THE EDOMITES (LEN SHATTOCK) 20

CHAPTER FIVE: THE PHILISTINES (T. BELTON) 31

CHAPTER SIX: THE EGYPTIANS (HENDY TAYLOR AND ARTHUR CHAMINGS) 36

CHAPTER SEVEN: THE ETHIOPIANS (D.W. MILLAR) 46

CHAPTER EIGHT: THE ASSYRIANS (J. RENFREW) 50

CHAPTER NINE: THE SYRIANS (DAVID JONES) 53

CHAPTER TEN: THE BABYLONIANS (LAURIE BURROWS AND PETER HICKLING) 60

CHAPTER ELEVEN: THE MEDO-PERSIANS (PETER HICKLING) 67

CHAPTER TWELVE: THE GIBEONITES (DR. A.T. DOODSON) 71

CHAPTER THIRTEEN: THE RECHABITES (DR. A.T. DOODSON) 76

CHAPTER FOURTEEN: THE RECHAHITES (DR. A.T. DOODSON) 81

CHAPTER FIFTEEN: THE CHERETHITES AND THE PELETHITES (DR. A.T. DOODSON)..................86

CHAPTER SIXTEEN: THE BONDSERVANTS OF SOLOMON (A.T. DOODSON)..................90

CHAPTER ONE: THE PHOENICIANS (GEORGE PRASHER)

Tyre and Sidon, two cities on the Phoenician seaboard north of Israel, are frequently linked in Biblical references. They stand for the great maritime power developed from Phoenicia, a power which reached out through its merchant and naval shipping to the far boundaries of the ancient world. Notice is taken of Tyre in the book of Joshua, for the border of Asher reached "to the fortified city of Tyre." (Joshua 19:29). Five hundred years later, as Joab reluctantly conducted the national census for David, he "came to Dan, and from Dan they went around to Sidon, 7 and came to the fortress of Tyre" (2 Samuel 24:6-7). So the influence of Tyre and Sidon, abutting the extreme northern border of Israel, was a political factor with which the kings of Israel and Judah were concerned. The four centuries from David until Jehoiakim saw the rise of Tyre and Sidon to the zenith of their influence and power.

Scripture discloses a cordial relationship between Hiram, King of Tyre, and David and Solomon. "Hiram always loved David" (1 Kings 5:1), and sent him cedars to provide material for his house (2 Chronicles 2:3). This economic co-operation was carried forward into Solomon's reign. Hiram supplied not only fir and cedar in return for wheat and oil (2 Chronicles 2:15-16), but also a highly skilled craftsman (2 Chronicles 2:13-14). This friendliness in the times of David and Solomon later gave place to enmity and rivalry. Allusions to Tyre and Sidon during the prophetic period under review were consistently in terms of judgement against them, often linked with references to their enmity against God's people. Why this change of attitudes? It may have derived from Hiram's disappointment in the cities of Galilee which

Solomon offered to him as a gift. For Hiram called them "land of Cabul" (meaning dry, sandy), and chided Solomon: "What kind of cities are these that you have given me, my brother?" (1 Kings 9:10-14).

Israel's hegemony of the middle eastern nations was broken after Solomon's death, when the predicted division of the kingdom came to pass. "This thing is of Me", were the LORD's words through the prophet to Rehoboam, and that word extended to the waning influence of Israel in relation to Tyre and Sidon as well as other countries. Nevertheless the very proximity of Tyre and Sidon to Israel's northern border encouraged trade relations. These are referred to in Ezekiel 27:17 - "Judah and the land of Israel traded with you; they exchanged for your merchandise wheat of Minnith, meal, honey, oil, and balm." Mutual distrust and conflicting interests would doubtless engender political and economic rivalry. Of Sidon it was later written, "there shall be no more a brier to prick or a thorn to hurt them among all their neighbors who have treated them with contempt. Then they will know that I am the Lord God." (Ezekiel 28:24).

The attitude of Tyre to Israel's discomfiture under the oppression of Assyrian and Chaldean invaders is significant: "Tyre said concerning Jerusalem, 'Aha, the gate of the peoples is broken; it has swung open to me. I shall be replenished, now that she is laid waste" (Ezekiel 26:2). Israel had commanded certain important trade routes from Tyre to other middle eastern areas, so her destruction was seen by Tyre as a political advantage.

Allusions to Tyre and Sidon in certain Old Testament prophetic books present a fascinating impression of the greatness to which they attained, and the foundation on which their greatness was built. Scriptural references accord convincingly with secular history's accounts of the Phoenician maritime empire, illustrating yet again the

THE NATIONS OF THE OLD TESTAMENT

vivid accuracy of the Old Testament prophets as they described the contemporary situation. Such references may be conveniently summarized under three headings:

1. Maritime Greatness

> "you who were inhabited from the seas, O city renowned, who was mighty on the sea" (Ezekiel 26:17).

> "Tyre, who dwells at the entrances to the sea, merchant of the peoples to many coastlands" (Ezekiel 27:3).

> "So you were filled and heavily laden in the heart of the seas" (Ezekiel 27:25).

2. Political Power

"Persia and Lud and Put were in your army as your men of war. They hung the shield and helmet in you; they gave you splendor. 11 Men of Arvad and Helech were on your walls all around, and men of Gamad were in your towers" (Ezekiel 27:10-11).

3. Material Wealth

> "Tyre ... heaped up silver like dust, and fine gold like the mud of the streets" (Zechariah 9:3).

> "Tarshish did business with you because of your great wealth of every kind...Many coastlands were your own special markets" (Ezekiel 27:12,15).

> "with your abundant wealth and merchandise you enriched the kings of the earth" (Ezekiel 27:33).

As with so many other gifted and prosperous peoples, power and wealth led Tyre to a state of overweening pride:

> "O Tyre, you have said, 'I am perfect in beauty'" (Ezekiel 27:3).

> "... you make your heart like the heart of a god" (Ezekiel 28:2).

So much so that by the inspiration of the Spirit Ezekiel was moved to reveal the pride and sin of Satan within the context of his burden regarding Tyre. For the prince of Tyre is represented as having a heart so lifted up in pride as to say, "'I am a god, I sit in the seat of the gods, in the heart of the seas," (Ezekiel 28:2), or as the Revised Version translates this: "... I sit in the seat of God." This lofty presumption in the rulers of contemporary Tyre is then projected back under the figure of the king of Tyre to the great crises of Satanic presumption against God, long before human history began:

> "raise a lamentation over the king of Tyre, and say to him, Thus says the Lord God: "You were the signet of perfection, full of wisdom and perfect in beauty ...You were an anointed guardian cherub ...Your heart was proud because of your beauty ... I cast you to the ground" (Ezekiel 28:12-19).

Here we find one of those masterpieces of divine revelation which command our awe and wonder. For through greatness and ability and power Tyre had been permitted to attain dazzling heights of human achievement. Forgetting that this was all of divine permission and enablement, she affronted God with her self-glorying. Here was an illustration in human experience through which God could convey to human thought the tragic elements of Satanic presumption against the prerogatives of Deity.

Religious Influences Upon Israel and Judah

There was a phase of Israel's experience when the false religion of the Phoenicians made serious inroads. This stemmed from a political move by Ahab, the son of Omri, who took Jezebel, the daughter of Ethbaal, king of the Zidonians, to be his wife (1 Kings 16:31). Was it with a view to political advantage that Ahab schemed to gain by association with the wealthy northern Phoenician power? His action was in defiance of God's word (Deuteronomy 7:3); it led Israel into even deeper spiritual decadence than what followed from the apostasy of Jeroboam the son of Nebat, originator of the worship of the golden calves in Dan and Bethel (2 Kings 13:11). For with Jezebel was imported the worship of Baal, chief male deity of the Phoenicians, and under the queen's forceful imposition the northern kingdom was soon given over to this religion.

Nor was that all. For Jehoshaphat, king of the southern kingdom of Judah, permitted the marriage of his son Jehoram to Athaliah, a daughter of Ahab (2 Chronicles 21:6). Jehoram's eight-year reign was a tragedy of apostasy and defeat; he "he departed with no one's regret". His son Ahaziah survived in kingship only one year, during which he "walked in the ways of the house of Ahab: for his mother was his counsellor in doing wickedly" (2 Chronicles 22:3). When he died, Athaliah destroyed all the seed royal of the house of Judah, assumed control of the kingdom, and further sponsored the Baal worship of the Zidonians. So the false religion of the Zidonians intruded to the heart of the Judean kingdom, to the very precincts of the house of God. The courage of Jehoiada and his wife in due course led to a coup d'etat which brought Joash to the throne and Athaliah to her ruin.

"... all the people went to the house of Baal and tore it down; his altars and his images they broke in pieces, and they killed Mattan the priest of Baal before the altars" (2 Chronicles 23:17). At such times of reformation the worship of Baal was suppressed in the kingdom of Judah, but it was never eradicated. More than a hundred years later the prophet Hosea declared: "I will punish her for the feast days of the Baals when she burned offerings to them" (Hosea 2:13); and when the Judean kingdom was finally hurtling towards the doom of the Chaldean invasion Jeremiah included this charge against her: "the people have forsaken me and have profaned this place by making offerings in it to other gods whom neither they nor their fathers nor the kings of Judah have known and because they have filled this place with the blood of innocents, and have built the high places of Baal to burn their sons in the fire as burnt offerings to Baal, which I did not command or decree, nor did it come into my mind" (Jeremiah 19:4-5).

Judgement on Tyre and Sidon Foretold

Several prophets foretold the decline and destruction of Tyre and Sidon, indicating that this would result from the hand of God in judgement. Isaiah 23 contains the prophet's burden concerning Tyre. He graphically depicts the discomfiture of Tarshish and Egypt, great trading centres in relation to Tyre, as they feel the impact of Tyre's destruction. "When the report comes to Egypt, they will be in anguish over the report about Tyre ... Who has purposed this against Tyre? ... The Lord of hosts has purposed it, to defile the pompous pride of all glory, to dishonor all the honored of the earth" (Isaiah 23:5,8-9).

Zechariah says of Tyre: "Behold, the Lord will dispossess her, and He will smite her power in the sea; and she shall be devoured with fire behold, the Lord will strip her of her possessions and strike down her power on the sea, and she shall be devoured by fire" (Zechariah 9:4). Jeremiah alludes to the cup of the wine of God's fury, which he was asked to take at the LORD's hand and make all the nations to drink it. Among them were "all the kings of Tyre, all the kings of Sidon" (Jeremiah 25:15-16, 22).

In Jeremiah 27:1-10 Jeremiah further included Tyre and Sidon among those who would be brought under the yoke of Nebuchadnezzar of Babylon. It was the prophet Ezekiel who was granted the fullest burden of judgement against these cities, a burden which comprises the whole of chapters 26, 27 and 28. To those who knew the power and greatness of Tyre it must have seemed incredible that she could be reduced so radically: "I will make you a bare rock. You shall be a place for the spreading of nets. You shall never be rebuilt, for I am the Lord; I have spoken, declares the Lord God" (Ezekiel 26:14). History records that Nebuchadnezzar captured the great stronghold after a thirteen years' siege. It was later rebuilt, but Alexander the Great conquered it after only seven months' siege. In due course the site of the original Tyre became literally but a place for the spreading of nets, a bare rock. As always, God had watched over His word to perform it.

End-Time Aspects

The prophets reveal that at the time of the end Tyre will again assume significance in relation to Israel. Joel 3:1-16 clearly points to the gathering of the nations for judgement at the coming of the Son of Man. Closely associated with that great crisis, we find Tyre and Sidon directly implicated in divine judgement because of their attitudes to Israel: "What are you to me, O Tyre and Sidon...I will return your payment on your own head swiftly and speedily. For you have taken my silver and my gold, and have carried my rich treasures into your temples.You have sold the people of Judah and Jerusalem ..." (Joel 3:4-6).

Psalm 83 also names the inhabitants of Tyre among the alliance of Israel's neighbouring powers with the avowed object of eliminating the holy people: "They say, "Come, let us wipe them out as a nation; let the name of Israel be remembered no more!" (Psalm 83:4). So in the prophetic picture of the Middle East at the time of the end, the coastal region of ancient Phoenicia is seen to be in solid alignment with the enemies of Israel, significant to a degree in the light of modern developments!

There is a remarkable word in Isaiah 23:18 which would seem to indicate a role for Tyre in the millennial kingdom. For after referring to the revival of Tyre as a centre of commerce, and to her playing the harlot with all the kingdoms of the world upon the face of the earth (verse 17), the prophet points to a dramatic reversal of that corrupt trend: "Her merchandise and her wages will be holy to the Lord. It will not be stored or hoarded, but her merchandise will supply abundant food and fine clothing for those who dwell before the Lord". Again in Psalm 45, which clearly looks forward to the glory of Messiah's triumph and reign, there is included the revealing word, "The people of Tyre will seek your favor with gifts, the richest of the people." (Psalm 45:12).

CHAPTER TWO: THE AMMONITES (C. MCKAY)

The origin of the nation of the Ammonites can be traced to the cave where Lot fled with his daughters after the destruction of Sodom and Gomorrah:

> "Now Lot went up out of Zoar and lived in the hills with his two daughters, for he was afraid to live in Zoar. So he lived in a cave with his two daughters. And the firstborn said to the younger, "Our father is old, and there is not a man on earth to come in to us after the manner of all the earth. Come, let us make our father drink wine, and we will lie with him, that we may preserve offspring from our father." So they made their father drink wine that night. And the firstborn went in and lay with her father. He did not know when she lay down or when she arose.
>
> The next day, the firstborn said to the younger, "Behold, I lay last night with my father. Let us make him drink wine tonight also. Then you go in and lie with him, that we may preserve offspring from our father." So they made their father drink wine that night also. And the younger arose and lay with him, and he did not know when she lay down or when she arose. Thus both the daughters of Lot became pregnant by their father. The firstborn bore a son and called his name Moab. He is the father of the Moabites to this day. The younger also bore a son and called his name Ben-ammi. He is the father of the Ammonites to this day" (Genesis 19:30-38).

It is evident that the licentious and immoral behaviour of these cities had a deadening effect upon their spiritual lives. The subsequent illicit union of these two women with their father clearly indicates that they had learned the evil practices of the cities of the plain. This resulted in the birth of a nation which was to become the age-long enemy of the people of Israel. The Ammonites settled near to their kindred race the Moabites, and their possession lay to the north of Moab stretching towards the river Jabbok (Deuteronomy 3:16). The eastern border of the tribe of Reuben was also the border of the Ammonites.

Chief Characteristics of the Ammonites and Their Impact on Israel

Persecution

Since the border between Israel and Ammon was common it is understandable that there would be frequent strife between the two nations. Ammon's defences were of prime consideration to them: "The border of the Ammonites was strong" (Numbers 21:24). They were an implacable foe who sought as occasion arose to enlarge their own borders at the expense of Israel. When the women of Gilead were with child they found themselves the victims of the knives of the Ammonites. The ultimate result was to reduce the nation's resistance to attack (Amos 1:13). Further evidence of the Ammonites' fierce incursions is to be found in 1 Samuel 11:2, when they sought to put out the right eyes of the men of Jabesh-Gilead and so bring them to a state of subservience.

Reproach

There was another method characteristic of Ammon, a tool to be used whenever the opportunity presented itself. The Lord showed His disapproval of them in their reproach of Israel in border disputes. Speaking through the prophet He said, "I have heard the ... the revilings of the Ammonites, how they have taunted my people and made boasts against their territory." (Zephaniah 2:8). After the return of the remnant from Babylon, when they built the wall of Jerusalem under the hand of Nehemiah, it was Tobiah the Ammonite who with the help of others heaped scorn on the builders. The book of Nehemiah reveals that it was Tobiah's intention to ridicule the work and make it appear of little consequence in the eyes of the remnant (Nehemiah 4:3).

Seduction

Outright persecution and reproach were not the only weapons in their armoury. They were also skilled in the art of seduction. When Solomon was king on the throne he fell prey to the women of the Ammonites. He forgot the words of his own proverb, "Keep your heart with all vigilance, for from it flow the springs of life". In old age his heart was drawn away after Milcom and Moloch the gods of the Ammonites (1 Kings 11:5-7). In the valley of Hinnom an altar to Moloch was set up and there the children of Israel participated in the terrible rites of human sacrifice setting aside the plain word of God which strictly forbade such practices (Leviticus 18:21).

Nehemiah in his day bemoaned the fact that the Jews had followed in the footsteps of Solomon in the matter of mixed marriages. The national language of the Israel nation was in danger of extinction as the offspring of the marriages spoke the language of the stranger, undoubtedly the outcome of the powerful influence of their strange parentage. Perhaps this was the most subtle tool used by this wily enemy.

The Place of Ammon in Prophecy

We have already mentioned how God took knowledge of the persecution of His people. Resulting judgement was foretold by the prophets. Sodom and Gomorrah always appear in the Word of God as typical of his terrible vengeance. Ammon is likened unto Gomorrah;

it would become a place of perpetual desolation and a possession of nettles and sand pits. "This shall be their lot in return for their pride" (Zephaniah 2:8-10), Rabbah was their chief city wherein was the bedstead of Og the king of Bashan (Deuteronomy 3:11). They had overcome men great and tall as the Anakim and had taken their city (Deuteronomy 2:21). But the Lord decreed through the prophet Amos that He would kindle a fire in the wall of Rabbah which would devour their palaces and their king would go into captivity (Amos 1:13-15). Jeremiah also prophesied of the day when Ammon would come under the yoke of Nebuchadnezzar:

> "Thus the Lord said to me: "Make yourself straps and yoke-bars, and put them on your neck. Send word to the king of Edom, the king of Moab, the king of the sons of Ammon, the king of Tyre, and the king of Sidon by the hand of the envoys who have come to Jerusalem to Zedekiah king of Judah. Give them this charge for their masters: 'Thus says the Lord of hosts, the God of Israel: This is what you shall say to your masters: "It is I who by my great power and my outstretched arm have made the earth, with the men and animals that are on the earth, and I give it to whomever it seems right to me. Now I have given all these lands into the hand of Nebuchadnezzar, the king of Babylon, my servant, and I have given him also the beasts of the field to serve him. All the nations shall serve him and his son and his grandson, until the time of his own land comes. Then many nations and great kings shall make him their slave.
>
> "'But if any nation or kingdom will not serve this Nebuchadnezzar king of Babylon, and put its neck under the yoke of the king of Babylon, I will punish that nation

with the sword, with famine, and with pestilence, declares the Lord, until I have consumed it by his hand" (Jeremiah 27:2-8).

In the prophecy of Ezekiel the Lord gives greater detail of the punishment of Ammon. Two ways were appointed for the king of Babylon, one for Jerusalem and one for Ammon. The king stood at the parting of the ways, and a sword was appointed for Ammon. The sword had already been in the hand of the furbisher "to cause it to devour, that it may be as lightning". It was ready to be use in the hand of Nebuchadnezzar who was skilled in the art of destruction. The Ammonites who were used to human sacrifice by fire, were soon to find themselves as fuel for its searing flame:

> "Mark a way for the sword to come to Rabbah of the Ammonites and to Judah, into Jerusalem the fortified. For the king of Babylon stands at the parting of the way, at the head of the two ways, to use divination. He shakes the arrows; he consults the teraphim; he looks at the liver. Into his right hand comes the divination for Jerusalem, to set battering rams, to open the mouth with murder, to lift up the voice with shouting, to set battering rams against the gates, to cast up mounds, to build siege towers. But to them it will seem like a false divination. They have sworn solemn oaths, but he brings their guilt to remembrance, that they may be taken.
>
> "Therefore thus says the Lord God: Because you have made your guilt to be remembered, in that your transgressions are uncovered, so that in all your deeds your sins appear - because you have come to remembrance, you shall be taken in hand. And you, O profane wicked one, prince of Israel, whose day has come, the time of your final punishment, thus

says the Lord God: Remove the turban and take off the crown. Things shall not remain as they are. Exalt that which is low, and bring low that which is exalted. A ruin, ruin, ruin I will make it. This also shall not be, until he comes, the one to whom judgment belongs, and I will give it to him.

"And you, son of man, prophesy, and say, Thus says the Lord God concerning the Ammonites and concerning their reproach; say, A sword, a sword is drawn for the slaughter. It is polished to consume and to flash like lightning ..." (Ezekiel 21:20-28).

Whatever the shape of the attack Ammon made on the people of Israel the Lord reveals the underlying motive behind it. In Ezekiel 25 the Lord said, "Son of Man ... prophesy against them. Say to the Ammonites, Hear the word of the Lord GOD ... Because you said, 'Aha!' over my sanctuary ..." The sanctuary of God was in the midst of Israel, and any persecution of the people of God in the day of their reproach was a reproach to the Lord God Himself. They stamped with the feet, they clapped their hands and rejoiced with all despite of their soul against the land of Israel. Therefore Rabbah would become a stable for camels and a couching place for flocks (Ezekiel 25:2-6).

CHAPTER THREE: THE MOABITES (JACK MCILVENNA)

When Lot lifted up his eyes and beheld all the Plain of Jordan that it was well watered everywhere and chose to dwell there, a train of events was set in motion which proved to be disastrous to Lot and his family, for he lost all that he hoped to preserve, and became the forefather of a nation that was to be the enemy of Israel in a day when they needed help. Spiritually Lot and his two daughters had reached a low ebb in the cave in the mountain above Zoar when those two women made a sinful pact and Lot allowed himself to become drunken with wine, resulting in their incestuous offspring, Moab and Ben-ammi. Moab, with whom our study is particularly concerned, was probably the more civilized half of Lot's descendants, and Ammon, the nation that sprung from Ben-ammi, the more fierce Bedouin-like half, because of the relationship between Abraham and Lot, was granted Moab, despite its beginning, became a nation of mighty men, and a special place amongst the nations, for to the Moabites was given Ar for a possession and Israel was instructed not to vex them, or to contend with them in battle (Deuteronomy 2:9).

These privileges were not valued by Moab, and so they failed to meet Israel with bread and water in the day of their need:

> "Moses sent messengers from Kadesh to the king of Edom: "Thus says your brother Israel: You know all the hardship that we have met: how our fathers went down to Egypt, and we lived in Egypt a long time. And the Egyptians dealt harshly with us and our fathers. And when we cried to the Lord, he heard our voice and sent an angel and brought us out of Egypt. And here we are in Kadesh, a city on the edge of your territory. Please let us pass through your land. We

will not pass through field or vineyard, or drink water from a well. We will go along the King's Highway. We will not turn aside to the right hand or to the left until we have passed through your territory."

"But Edom said to him, "You shall not pass through, lest I come out with the sword against you." And the people of Israel said to him, "We will go up by the highway, and if we drink of your water, I and my livestock, then I will pay for it. Let me only pass through on foot, nothing more." But he said, "You shall not pass through." And Edom came out against them with a large army and with a strong force. Thus Edom refused to give Israel passage through his territory, so Israel turned away from him" (Numbers 20:14-21; see also Judges 11:17).

Edom acted in a like fashion, as a result of which Israel was caused to take a circuitous route round these two kingdoms. When Israel pitched in the plain of Moab beyond the Jordan, trembling took hold of the mighty men of Moab, for they feared this people because of what they had done to the Amorites. So great was Moab's fear that Balak the son of Zippor, king of Moab, confessed that Israel was too mighty for him, and so he sought an alternative means of overcoming them by hiring Balaam that he might curse Israel and enable him to drive them out of the land.

But Balak learned on that occasion that it is impossible to curse when God has not cursed, or defy when the LORD has not defied, and so Israel received a three-fold blessing, for the LORD their God loved them, and to Balak was revealed what Israel would do to Moab in the latter days (Numbers 24:17).

Within a short time the anger of the LORD was kindled against Israel, for some of their number began to associate with the Moabites, having been called to partake in the sacrifices to their gods. A similar happening took place in the days of Solomon when his heart was turned away after other gods by his strange wives, and he built a high place for Chemosh the abomination of Moab in the mount that is before Jerusalem, as a result of which the kingdom was divided in the days of Rehoboam (1 Kings 11:12), Thus Moab was more successful in spiritual assaults on Israel than in actual physical onslaught.

Moab was not permitted to sin against God's people with impunity, for as a result of their acts it was commanded that they would not enter into the assembly of the LORD, even to the tenth generation, and Israel from henceforth was not to seek their peace nor their prosperity for ever:

> "No Ammonite or Moabite may enter the assembly of the Lord. Even to the tenth generation, none of them may enter the assembly of the Lord forever, because they did not meet you with bread and with water on the way, when you came out of Egypt, and because they hired against you Balaam the son of Beor from Pethor of Mesopotamia, to curse you. But the Lord your God would not listen to Balaam; instead the Lord your God turned the curse into a blessing for you, because the Lord your God loved you. You shall not seek their peace or their prosperity all your days forever" (Deuteronomy 23:3-6).

After this there was strife between the two nations, sometimes because of Israel's sin when God used Moab to punish His people. This was the case in the days of Eglon, when God strengthened Moab against them and caused their cities to be occupied, and Israel to be brought into bondage for eighteen years (Judges 3:12-14).

On other occasions it was Israel who were the assailants, as in the early days of the reign of Saul when he sought to establish himself in his kingdom by fighting against his enemies on every side (1 Samuel 14:47). David too, fought against the Moabites. He subdued them, and they became servants to him, and the silver and gold which he won from them was dedicated to the LORD (1 Chronicles 18:11).

Nevertheless the grace of God is seen on more than one occasion in regard to this nation, for of them there were some who found a place amongst the people of God. Doubtless when Ruth the Moabitess met the Ephrathite family of Bethlehem-Judah, she did not dream that this was the beginning of an association which would eventually lead to her being the wife of Boaz and being listed in the book of the genealogy of Jesus Christ. Because of her great desire that she should stand in the same relationship to God and Naomi's people as Naomi herself, and shelter under the wings of the LORD, the God of Israel, the LORD recompensed her. She became the wife of Boaz the mighty man of wealth, and the mother of Obed the father of Jesse, the father of David, and her name is eternally recorded in the genealogy of Jesus Christ (Ruth 1:16, 2:11-12, 4:9-10,17; Matthew 1:1,5).

Ithmah, the Moabite, is another who is given a place of special mention, being listed as one of David's mighty men (1 Chronicles 11:46). Nevertheless, Moab was characteristically a people who trusted in their works and in their treasures. Their pride and arrogancy and the haughtiness of their hearts were well known. Despite the fact that God had granted them a favoured place in a good land, so that they were able to be at ease from their youth, they attributed their place to their own right and magnified themselves against the LORD; Israel they regarded with derision, as evidenced in the following verses: Jeremiah 48:1,7,14,26, 27,29; Ezekiel 25:5.

It is recorded in the words of the Preacher, son of David, king of Jerusalem, that because sentence against an evil work is not executed speedily, therefore the heart of the sons of men is emboldened in them to do evil (Ecclesiastes 8:11, RV margin). This was verily true of Moab, of whom the LORD said through His prophet Amos, "For three transgressions of Moab, and for four, I will not revoke the punishment" (Amos 2:1-2), and Isaiah prophesied that the judgement would be fulfilled within three years, when in a night Ar of Moab and Kir of Moab would be laid waste and brought to nought (Isaiah 15:1-4). Jeremiah too, prophesied of judgement, which judgement was performed by Nebuchadnezzar, for to him was given their land and their beasts of the field to serve him and his son and his son's son.

But the LORD promised that he would bring about the captivity of Moab in the latter days (Jeremiah 48:47), and so when the king of the North (Daniel 11) sweeps down to conquer the king of the South, Moab, the old enemy of Israel, will escape judgement, for they are to be numbered amongst Israel's enemies at the time of the great regathering for the reign of the One whose Name is the Branch. Then will follow the judgement of Moab by Israel, when they will put forth their hand upon Edom and Moab and the children of Ammon will obey them (Isaiah 11:14).

CHAPTER FOUR: THE EDOMITES (LEN SHATTOCK)

The name Edom was derived from Esau (Genesis 36:1) and is applied both to the descendants of Esau (Numbers 20:20-21) and to the country in which they lived (Jeremiah 49:17). Geographically it was a mountainous range and as such it provided natural rocky fortresses against enemy attack. It stretched from the Dead Sea to the Red Sea. In the north it bordered with Judah and Moab and in the south with Midian and the desert of Sinai. Among its towns mentioned in Scripture are Dinhabah, Bozrah, Teman, Avith, Pau (Genesis 36:32-39) and Ezion-geber (1 Kings 9:26).

Most important of all was Sela - the rock (2 Kings 14:7), now identified as Petra, its Greek name having the same meaning. It was approached on one side by a chasm so narrow that no more than two horsemen could ride abreast through it and on the other side by an ascent so steep as to daunt any who would consider assailing it. It is not surprising, therefore, that when Amaziah captured it he changed its name to Joktheel, which means "yielded by God", although despite this implied recognition of the Lord giving him victory the same king adopted the idolatrous worship of the Edomites (2 Chronicles 25:14).

Prior to its occupation by the descendants of Esau, Edom was called Mount Seir (Genesis 32:3) and its original inhabitants were the Horites (Deuteronomy 2:12). The Greek equivalent of Edom is Idumaea, but the New Testament reference (Mark 3:8) is to an extended land area annexed by the Edomite exploitation of the defeat of Judah by the Babylonians. Kings were appointed in Edom "before there reigned any king over the children of Israel ..." but the turbulent nature of the Edomite is perhaps shown by the fact that none of their kingships passed from father to son:

"These are the kings who reigned in the land of Edom, before any king reigned over the Israelites. Bela the son of Beor reigned in Edom, the name of his city being Dinhabah. Bela died, and Jobab the son of Zerah of Bozrah reigned in his place. Jobab died, and Husham of the land of the Temanites reigned in his place. Husham died, and Hadad the son of Bedad, who defeated Midian in the country of Moab, reigned in his place, the name of his city being Avith. Hadad died, and Samlah of Masrekah reigned in his place. Samlah died, and Shaul of Rehoboth on the Euphrates[b] reigned in his place. Shaul died, and Baal-hanan the son of Achbor reigned in his place. Baal-hanan the son of Achbor died, and Hadar reigned in his place, the name of his city being Pau; his wife's name was Mehetabel, the daughter of Matred, daughter of Mezahab" (Genesis 36:31-39).

Nonetheless, in the days of Solomon's defection from the God of Israel an adversary raised up against him was "Hadad the Edomite. He was of the royal house in Edom" (1 Kings 11:14).

"You shall not abhor an Edomite, for he is your brother" (Deuteronomy 23:7). Considered in the light of the statement "Jacob I loved, but Esau I hated" (Romans 9:13, Malachi 1:2-5), this may seem difficult to understand unless careful consideration is given to the righteous principles which underlie both statements. The Israelite was to harbour no contempt for the Edomite because he was the descendant of Esau the brother of Jacob, the father of the nation of Israel. On the other hand, Israel were the people of God and as such governed by divine truth diametrically opposed to that pattern of life which characterized Esau and Edomites.

Israel's separation from Edom was in no way to be relaxed because of the commandment of Deuteronomy 23:7. Moreover it cannot be argued that Jacob and Esau, either in their individual or national characters, became what they were because God loved or hated them. Rather it is true that God's love or hatred resulted from what they were and what their character was. Esau was a profane person (Hebrews 12:16) - a man who despised spiritual values. The attitude of life which he represented was perpetuated in his descendants, who were characterized by arrant self-sufficiency and pride (Obadiah 1:3).

The antagonism of Esau and Jacob and that of their posterity were prefigured before their birth. The wrestling of the unborn children of Rebekah was declared by God to be reflective of the bitter opposition which would exist between Israel and Edom (Genesis 25:23).

Historically this found expression in:

> (1) Edom's refusal to allow Israel, at the time of the Exodus, to pass through their land on the way to Canaan (Numbers 20:18);
>
> (2) King Saul having to contend with Edomites, among others, who threatened the security of his kingdom (1 Samuel 14:47);
>
> (3) King David needing to establish garrisons in Edomite cities (2 Samuel 8:14);
>
> (4) Edom being among the named enemies of God who were allied in the common purpose that "the name of Israel be remembered no more" (Psalm 83:4).

The record of 2 Chronicles 20 is considered by some scholars to describe the circumstances which prompted the writing of Psalm 83. Each views the same confederacy in which Edom was involved (2 Chronicles 20:10; Psalm 83:6-7), and each declares the fact which is sustained throughout the sacred writings that, in their opposition to Israel, the Edomites were the enemies of God (2 Chronicles 20:11; Psalm 83:5).

The Bible student is left with a terrible picture of Edom's cruelty and violence to Israel. Obadiah tells us how the Edomite, from his high mountain fortresses, watched in aloof and gloating delight the sufferings of God's people and then in the day of calamity entered the cities of Judaea and robbed Jacob of his substance. From the land of their exile the Jewish captives asked the LORD to remember the part Edom played at the fall of Jerusalem, and to recall that then the Edomite cry was "Lay it bare, lay it bare, down to its foundations" (Psalm 137:7).

It is against this background of cruelty and hate that we must read the prophetic utterances of judgement contained in such scriptures as Jeremiah 49:7-22:

> "Concerning Edom. Thus says the Lord of hosts: "Is wisdom no more in Teman? Has counsel perished from the prudent? Has their wisdom vanished? Flee, turn back, dwell in the depths, O inhabitants of Dedan! For I will bring the calamity of Esau upon him, the time when I punish him. If grape gatherers came to you, would they not leave gleanings? If thieves came by night, would they not destroy only enough for themselves? But I have stripped Esau bare; I have uncovered his hiding places, and he is not able to conceal himself.

His children are destroyed, and his brothers, and his neighbors; and he is no more. Leave your fatherless children; I will keep them alive; and let your widows trust in me." For thus says the Lord: "If those who did not deserve to drink the cup must drink it, will you go unpunished? You shall not go unpunished, but you must drink. For I have sworn by myself, declares the Lord, that Bozrah shall become a horror, a taunt, a waste, and a curse, and all her cities shall be perpetual wastes." I have heard a message from the Lord, and an envoy has been sent among the nations: "Gather yourselves together and come against her, and rise up for battle! For behold, I will make you small among the nations, despised among mankind. The horror you inspire has deceived you, and the pride of your heart, you who live in the clefts of the rock, who hold the height of the hill.

Though you make your nest as high as the eagle's, I will bring you down from there, declares the Lord. "Edom shall become a horror. Everyone who passes by it will be horrified and will hiss because of all its disasters. As when Sodom and Gomorrah and their neighboring cities were overthrown, says the Lord, no man shall dwell there, no man shall sojourn in her. Behold, like a lion coming up from the jungle of the Jordan against a perennial pasture, I will suddenly make him run away from her. And I will appoint over her whomever I choose. For who is like me? Who will summon me? What shepherd can stand before me?

Therefore hear the plan that the Lord has made against Edom and the purposes that he has formed against the inhabitants of Teman: Even the little ones of the flock shall be dragged away. Surely their fold shall be appalled at their fate. At the sound of their fall the earth shall tremble; the

THE NATIONS OF THE OLD TESTAMENT

sound of their cry shall be heard at the Red Sea. Behold, one shall mount up and fly swiftly like an eagle and spread his wings against Bozrah, and the heart of the warriors of Edom shall be in that day like the heart of a woman in her birth pains" (see also Lamentations 4:21: Ezekiel 25:12,44; Ezekiel 35; Joel 3:19).

Edom's arrogance was reflected in his boast "Who will bring me down?" (Obadiah 1:3) to which the LORD replied "I will bring thee down ..." (Jeremiah 49:16) – "As you have done, it shall be done to you" (Obadiah 1:15). The story of Edom emphasizes how inescapable are the consequences of defiance of God, and witness clearly to the truth, "whatever one sows, that will he also reap." (Galatians 6:7; Matthew 7:2).

The site of the fortress city of Petra can still be viewed today. The casual tourist may see it as a reflection of a bygone age, but to the spiritually sensitive its ruined palaces, overgrown with briars and weeds, its desolation except for the presence of wild goats and birds, demonstrate the clear fulfilment of scriptural prophecy (Isaiah 34:5-17) and the certainty of divine judgement:

> "For my sword has drunk its fill in the heavens;
>
> behold, it descends for judgment upon Edom,
>
> upon the people I have devoted to destruction.
>
> The Lord has a sword; it is sated with blood;
>
> it is gorged with fat,
>
> with the blood of lambs and goats,
>
> with the fat of the kidneys of rams.

For the Lord has a sacrifice in Bozrah,

a great slaughter in the land of Edom.

Wild oxen shall fall with them,

and young steers with the mighty bulls.

Their land shall drink its fill of blood,

and their soil shall be gorged with fat.

For the Lord has a day of vengeance,

a year of recompense for the cause of Zion.

And the streams of Edom shall be turned into pitch,

and her soil into sulfur;

her land shall become burning pitch.

Night and day it shall not be quenched;

its smoke shall go up forever.

From generation to generation it shall lie waste;

none shall pass through it forever and ever.

But the hawk and the porcupine shall possess it,

the owl and the raven shall dwell in it.

He shall stretch the line of confusion over it,

and the plumb line of emptiness.

Its nobles—there is no one there to call it a kingdom,

and all its princes shall be nothing.

Thorns shall grow over its strongholds,

nettles and thistles in its fortresses.

It shall be the haunt of jackals,

an abode for ostriches.

And wild animals shall meet with hyenas;

the wild goat shall cry to his fellow;

indeed, there the night bird settles

and finds for herself a resting place.

There the owl nests and lays

and hatches and gathers her young in her shadow;

indeed, there the hawks are gathered,

each one with her mate.

Seek and read from the book of the Lord:

Not one of these shall be missing;

none shall be without her mate.

For the mouth of the Lord has commanded,

and his Spirit has gathered them.

He has cast the lot for them;

his hand has portioned it out to them with the line;

they shall possess it forever;

from generation to generation they shall dwell in it."

Today men are still dominated by minds that have no spiritual concepts, like Esau and the Edomites, having no vision of the unseen in arrant pride reflecting attitudes which declare "Who shall bring me down?" The ultimate expression of this will be in a confederate rebellion against the LORD and against His anointed, as depicted in Revelation 16:14; 17:3,12-14:

> "For they are demonic spirits, performing signs, who go abroad to the kings of the whole world, to assemble them for battle on the great day of God the Almighty ... And he carried me away in the Spirit into a wilderness, and I saw a woman sitting on a scarlet beast that was full of blasphemous names, and it had seven heads and ten horns ... And the ten horns that you saw are ten kings who have not yet received royal power, but they are to receive authority as kings for one hour, together with the beast. These are of one mind, and they hand over their power and authority to the beast. They will make war on the Lamb, and the Lamb will conquer them, for he is Lord of lords and King of kings, and those with him are called and chosen and faithful."

It will be a rebellion which also will include in its aims that Israel should be cut off from being a nation (Psalm 83:4). Then the cry, "Who is this that cometh from Edom with dyed garments from Bozrah?" will herald the revelation of the divine Conqueror, mighty to save who having trod the winepress of judgement:

"Who is this who comes from Edom,

in crimsoned garments from Bozrah,

he who is splendid in his apparel,

marching in the greatness of his strength?

"It is I, speaking in righteousness,

mighty to save."

Why is your apparel red,

and your garments like his who treads in the winepress?

"I have trodden the winepress alone,

and from the peoples no one was with me;

I trod them in my anger

and trampled them in my wrath;

their lifeblood spattered on my garments,

and stained all my apparel.

For the day of vengeance was in my heart,

and my year of redemption had come.

I looked, but there was no one to help;

I was appalled, but there was no one to uphold;

so my own arm brought me salvation,

and my wrath upheld me.

I trampled down the peoples in my anger;

I made them drunk in my wrath,

and I poured out their lifeblood on the earth." (Isaiah 63:1-6).

And so He will establish that final triumph which ends the prophecy of Obadiah. "The kingdom shall be the Lord's".

CHAPTER FIVE: THE PHILISTINES (T. BELTON)

Geographical Situation

Philistia, the land of the Philistines, lay along the western flank of Judah, sitting astride the land corridor that ran between Egypt and Syria and is known today as the Gaza Strip. From ancient times Philistia was on the highway between the great nations lying to the north and south of the land of Israel and it was strategically important to them. The boundaries of the land were the Mediterranean from Gaza to Jaffa on the west; the plain of Sharon on the north; the hills of Judah on the east; and the Egyptian desert in the south. Its five great cities of Gaza, Ashdod, Ashkelon, Ekron and Gath (1 Samuel 6:17) were fortresses built to withstand attacks from north or south and it is recorded that Ashdod withstood the might of the Egyptian army for 29 years, the longest siege on record.

The land was very fertile and its produce, together with the revenues from the caravan traffic along the coastal road, made the Philistines a powerful and prosperous nation. They were renowned as skilful mariners, and no doubt sea-going trade brought more wealth into their coffers. In addition, they excelled in the smelting of iron and in its uses for both peaceful and warlike purposes.

History

It appears that the Philistines came originally from the Aegean; moving by stages to Crete, anciently known as Caphtorim (from which they gained their early name), they came to Cyprus and then to the coastland of Palestine, which itself received its name from the Philistines. There they established themselves after several invasions at different times from the days of Abraham until the Exodus of the children of Israel from Egypt. The land of the Philistines and their five principal cities are mentioned in the book of Joshua (13:3) as land that still remained to be possessed, but Israel never succeeded in doing this, although Judah for a time captured the cities of Gaza, Ashkelon and Ekron.

In the book of Judges (Judges 3:3-4), God expressly states that He was leaving the five lords of the Philistines with others to teach the children of Israel war and to know whether they would hearken unto the commandments of the Lord. They remained there as a constant thorn in the side of Judah until she was finally taken captive into Babylon. God finally punished Philistia and her inhabitants for her unrelenting hostility towards Israel and particularly for her treachery in the time of His people's greatest need when Israel's land was invaded and overrun by the armies of the Chaldeans. He brought about the sacking of her cities and the pillaging of the land by Nebuchadnezzar and completed His vengeance when Alexander the Great swept through the land, razing their cities and depopulating the country (Zephaniah 2:4-6) so that no trace of Philistine occupation remains today:

> "For Gaza shall be deserted, and Ashkelon shall become a desolation; Ashdod's people shall be driven out at noon, and Ekron shall be uprooted. Woe to you inhabitants of the seacoast, you nation of the Cherethites! The word of the Lord is against you, O Canaan, land of the Philistines; and I will destroy you until no inhabitant is left. And you, O seacoast, shall be pastures, with meadows for shepherds and folds for flocks."

Influence Upon Israel

THE NATIONS OF THE OLD TESTAMENT

Unlike the Edomites or the Moabites and the children of Ammon, there existed no blood relationship between the Philistines and Israel, for the Philistines were descendants of Ham. As we noted in Judges, they were left close at hand to Israel so that their idolatrous worship and soothsaying, and the evil practices that go along with these things, should test her faithfulness to God, and there they remained, a constant source of attraction to pleasure-loving Israelites. Samson, the one-time saviour of Israel, consorted with Delilah, and was finally bound by his enemies. With eyes put out he was made sport of before the rejoicing crowds of Philistines. Such is the humiliation that the enemies of God can bring to His people.

After this, in the early days of Saul's reign, the Philistines dominated Israel. Permission had to be asked to sharpen any cutting instrument such as an axe or ploughshare. David on the other hand, always appreciated the true character of the Philistines. When he did battle with the giant, he did not rely on his own prowess, but on the help of the Lord. Later, in the destroying of Ziklag by the Amalekites and the capture of his wives and his friends' dependents, he learned not to compromise with the enemy and afterwards declared unceasing war upon them until they should trouble him no more.

Prophetic Denunciations of Philistia

God was not unmindful of the continual hatred of the Philistines for His people, stemming possibly from the fact that Israel had taken much of the land of Palestine which they considered belonged to them, and He foretold their ultimate destruction. In the days of Ahaz king of Judah who associated himself and his people with the vile idolatrous practices of the nations surrounding his land, God beset Judah with enemies on all sides, even allowing the king of Israel to invade the land and take many of the people captive.

The Philistines saw this as their opportunity to avenge their defeats at the hands of David in past years. Entering the land they took the cities of Beth-shemesh, Aijalon Gederoth, Soco and Timnah (2 Chronicles 28:18). Both Jeremiah and Amos denounce this treacherous act. Jeremiah says:

> "Thus saith the LORD: Behold, waters rise up out of the north, and shall become an overflowing stream, and shall overflow the land and all that is therein, the city and them that dwell therein: ... because of the day that cometh to spoil all the Philistines, to cut off from Tyre and Zidon every helper that remaineth: for the LORD will spoil the Philistines, the remnant of the isle of Caphtor. Baldness is come upon Gaza; Ashkelon is brought to nought"

"Thus says the Lord: Behold, waters are rising out of the north, and shall become an overflowing torrent; they shall overflow the land and all that fills it, the city and those who dwell in it. ... because of the day that is coming to destroy all the Philistines, to cut off from Tyre and Sidon every helper that remains. For the Lord is destroying the Philistines, the remnant of the coastland of Caphtor. Baldness has come upon Gaza; Ashkelon has perished. (Jeremiah 47:2-5).

Amos speaks of the ultimate destruction of the Philistines:

> "Thus says the Lord: "For three transgressions of Gaza, and for four, I will not revoke the punishment, because they carried into exile a whole people to deliver them up to Edom. So I will send a fire upon the wall of Gaza, and it shall devour her strongholds. I will cut off the inhabitants from Ashdod, and him who holds the scepter from Ashkelon; I will turn my hand against Ekron, and the remnant of the Philistines shall perish," says the Lord God." (Amos 1:6-8).

THE NATIONS OF THE OLD TESTAMENT 35

So the armies of Nebuchadnezzar swept down from the north, ravaging the country of the Philistines and isolating Tyre and Zidon from their last ally, preparatory to the destruction of these two great cities, foretold in the prophecy of Ezekiel. Finally, Zechariah has to say that Ashkelon and Gaza, seeing the destruction of Tyre, will, together with other Philistine cities be destroyed but: "I will take away its blood from its mouth, and its abominations from between its teeth; it too shall be a remnant for our God; it shall be like a clan in Judah, and Ekron shall be like the Jebusites" (Zechariah 9:5-7).

Despite the predictions of punishment and near extirpation of the race of the Philistines, here is a promise that God will one day give them a place alongside Israel in the coming Millennium, when they will be taught no more to eat blood or food sacrificed to idols, which is abominable to the Lord. They will, it seems, occupy a similar position of inferiority as did the Jebusites in the time of David.

CHAPTER SIX: THE EGYPTIANS (HENDY TAYLOR AND ARTHUR CHAMINGS)

Influences on Israel During the Prophetic Period

In examining Israel's historical background, the striking phenomenon is the rise, fall and disappearance of several great world empires - Egypt, Assyria, Babylonia, Persia, Greece and Rome, and withal the survival of the Jews; not, it is true as a complete nation but as a distinct racial unity living through the vicissitudes of exile, subjection, persecution and independence. At the end of it all, though crushed and scattered, they remained virile and indestructible. There is no doubt however that a major impact on the life of the nation of Israel over its past history was that of the enduring menace of the Egyptian regime.

The prophets that form the basis of our current study lived between the years 850-550 B.C., approximately. Listed below are some of the major historical events recorded in the Scriptures relating to Egypt's activities against the people of God.

- 930 B.C.: Shishak invades Judaea and takes the treasures of Jerusalem (1 Kin.14:25; 2 Chron.12:2-9)
- 916 B.C.: Invasion of Judah by Zerah the Ethiopian (2 Chron.14:9-15; 2 Chron. 16:8)
- 722 B.C.: Alliance with Hoshea king of Israel (2 Kin.17.4)
- 610 B.C.: Pharaoh-neco's war with Israel - Death of Josiah (2 Chron.35:20-27)
- 605 B.C.: Pharaoh-neco defeated by Nebuchadnezzar (Jer.46:1-2; Ezek.29:19-20; Ezek.32:31)
- 581 B.C.: Nebuchadnezzar deposes Pharaoh Hophra (Jer.44:30; Ezek.31:18)

Mizraim (son of Ham) was colonized by the descendants of Ham, but the first recorded point of contact between Egypt and Israel is that in Genesis 12:10: "Now there was a famine in the land. So Abram went down to Egypt to sojourn there, for the famine was severe in the land." Of the spiritual consequences of this move there can be no mistake, and the influences resulting from such association form the fundamental pattern in the disastrous effects upon Israel throughout these vital years of prophetic history.

One of the most traumatic experiences of the Israelites in all their history was their stay in Egypt resulting from Joseph's rise to power and from Jacob going to live in Goshen. 1 Kings 6:1 indicates that the building of the temple in the fourth year of Solomon's reign took place 480 years after the exodus. Such references as Joel 3:19, Micah 6:4, 7:15 clearly indicate the significance of the exodus and God's calling of a nation for His own possession out of a land where culture and worldly ambitions had so forcibly made their imprint on the lives of His people.

> "Egypt shall become a desolation and Edom a desolate wilderness, for the violence done to the people of Judah, because they have shed innocent blood in their land" (Joel 3:19).

> "For I brought you up from the land of Egypt and redeemed you from the house of slavery, and I sent before you Moses, Aaron, and Miriam" (Micah 6:4).

A continual reminder of God's redemptive work - "remember that you were a slave in Egypt and the Lord your God redeemed you from there; therefore I command you to do this." (Deuteronomy 24:18) - should have had the salutary effect of humbling their minds; and the prophets were undaunted in their efforts to achieve this end. Paul's words to the Corinthians have a solemn meaning to us; "for you were bought with a price. So glorify God in your body" (1 Corinthians 6:20).

The period of the Judges and the early part of the Israel monarchy provide no mention of Egypt. With the accession of Solomon, however, a period of alliance was re-established. 1 Kings 3:1 indicates that "Solomon made affinity with Pharaoh king of Egypt, and took Pharaoh's daughter, and brought her into the city of David". The wedding gift that the king of Egypt gave to his daughter is of considerable importance – "Gezer ... as dowry to his daughter, Solomon's wife" (1 Kings 9:16). Gezer was one of the towns from which the Israelites had never succeeded in dislodging the Canaanites (Judges 1:29), and after Solomon's death, the Egyptians, having secured this flank in the wasted plain, invaded Judah through Shishak, the first Egyptian ruler of the Libyan 22nd Dynasty (2 Chronicles 12:2).

The extravagances and excesses of Egypt began to find their place in the lives of the leading classes of Israel. Throughout the history of the divided monarchy there is abundant evidence as to the level of this prosperity. Contemporary prophets, such as Amos and Isaiah, spoke gravely of this menace to Israel's spiritual welfare as in Isaiah 5: 11-12 and Amos 6:1-8:

> "Woe to those who rise early in the morning, that they may run after strong drink, who tarry late into the evening as wine inflames them! They have lyre and harp, tambourine and flute and wine at their feasts, but they do not regard the deeds of the Lord, or see the work of his hands" (Isaiah 5:11-12).

"Woe to those who are at ease in Zion, and to those who feel secure on the mountain of Samaria, the notable men of the first of the nations, to whom the house of Israel comes! Pass over to Calneh, and see, and from there go to Hamath the great; then go down to Gath of the Philistines. Are you better than these kingdoms? Or is their territory greater than your territory, O you who put far away the day of disaster and bring near the seat of violence?

"Woe to those who lie on beds of ivory and stretch themselves out on their couches, and eat lambs from the flock and calves from the midst of the stall, who sing idle songs to the sound of the harp and like David invent for themselves instruments of music, who drink wine in bowls and anoint themselves with the finest oils, but are not grieved over the ruin of Joseph! Therefore they shall now be the first of those who go into exile, and the revelry of those who stretch themselves out shall pass away." The Lord God has sworn by himself, declares the Lord, the God of hosts: "I abhor the pride of Jacob and hate his strongholds, and I will deliver up the city and all that is in it" (Amos 6:1-8).

Apart from the Rechabites and Nazirites the people became oblivious to the perils in which the nation stood and the prophets felt they must exercise the profoundest influence in seeking to draw them back to God and the divine principles which underlay the Covenant. Through faith their critical faculties were unimpaired and undimmed by the existing evils of their generation. The God of Israel demanded fair and righteous dealings amongst His people, and that which was morally evil to the prophets could not possibly be pleasing to Him. Isaiah's utterances to the people on the subject of Egyptian alliance are vigorous and contemptuous. In Isaiah 19:1 a pronouncement of doom is made against Egypt, and in chapter 30 Egypt is again bitterly denounced. Trust in Egypt would be the shame and reproach of Judah. Compare also with this the words of Rabshakeh in 2 Kings 18:21: "Behold, you are trusting now in Egypt, that broken reed of a staff, which will pierce the hand of any man who leans on it".

Again in Isaiah 31:1-3 there is a further denunciation of the pro-Egyptian policy:

> "Woe to those who go down to Egypt for help and rely on horses, who trust in chariots because they are many and in horsemen because they are very strong, but do not look to the Holy One of Israel or consult the Lord! And yet he is wise and brings disaster; he does not call back his words, but will arise against the house of the evildoers and against the helpers of those who work iniquity. The Egyptians are man, and not God, and their horses are flesh, and not spirit. When the Lord stretches out his hand, the helper will stumble, and he who is helped will fall, and they will all perish together."

To the prophet, God was holy and His people must be holy. To secure this end it was needful to be separate from the other nations. Egypt in particular was a nation that stood in contrast and opposition to all that was for God - flesh as opposed to spirit - and Judah must not be allowed to be contaminated by close association with Egypt. Isaiah's call must find a place in our hearts, for wholehearted consecration to God is the paramount demand upon us. Egypt's influence on Israel during the time of the prophets reached its climax when in 605 B.C. the battle of Carchemish saw the defeat of Pharaoh-neco by Nebuchadnezzar, Jeremiah perhaps the noblest prophet of all, realised the significance of the battle, and his account of the overthrow is both lucid and vivid.

He saw that this defeat would put an end to Egypt's hopes of further world dominance (Jeremiah 46:3-12). Then followed the invasion of Israel by the Chaldean army under the direction of Nebuchadnezzar, the destruction of Jerusalem and the subsequent placing of Zedekiah on the throne. Zedekiah was essentially a weak man and few words in the Old Testament carry a deeper pathos than his reply to the princes who demanded that Jeremiah should be put to death. "The king can do nothing against you" (Jeremiah 38:5).

From Jeremiah's account there appears to have been two sectional interests in Israel, pro-Babylonian and pro-Egyptian. With the rise of Hophra in Egypt support was given to a further invasion, but the Egyptians were decisively beaten (Jeremiah 44:30). To the survivors the position was desperate, and led by Johanon they determined to make their way to Egypt although they consulted Jeremiah (chapter 42), who, after seeking God's face for ten days, forbade them to go. They disregarded Jeremiah's word and took him with them despite his strong protests (2 Kings 25-26). This was the break-up of the Israelite nation as a political entity as is clearly indicated in Jeremiah 44:26-28:

> "Therefore hear the word of the Lord, all you of Judah who dwell in the land of Egypt: Behold, I have sworn by my great name, says the Lord, that my name shall no more be invoked by the mouth of any man of Judah in all the land of Egypt, saying, 'As the Lord God lives.' Behold, I am watching over them for disaster and not for good. All the men of Judah who are in the land of Egypt shall be consumed by the sword and by famine, until there is an end of them. And those who escape the sword shall return from the land of Egypt to the land of Judah, few in number; and all the remnant of Judah, who came to the land of Egypt to live, shall know whose word will stand, mine or theirs."

From the perusal of the Scriptural record, without controversy or exception, the effect of Egyptian influence was harmful to God's ancient people. Egypt is a clear type of the world. Its land was near to the land of God's choice. Let us not lose the spiritual import both in our personal lives and in collective testimony as the Israel of God. "Do not love the world" (1 John 2:15-17).

Prophetic Aspects of Egypt's Destiny

Egypt, an advanced civilisation when Abraham came out of Ur of the Chaldees, is spoken of in Scripture from Genesis to Revelation and, apart from Israel, is referred to in the divine record more than any other nation. Perhaps the first and last references to Egypt epitomise the contrast of the spiritual and the natural, for Abraham "went down to Egypt" (Genesis 12:10); and the ultimate sin of Israel in the rejection of Messiah provoked the divine reproach against "the great city that symbolically is called Sodom and Egypt, where their Lord was crucified" (Revelation 11:8).

Immediately adjacent to the Holy Land, Egypt's fortunes have run parallel with those of Israel for the four thousand years or more of Jewish history, prior to which Egypt had produced some of the world's structural masterpieces in its pyramids and mighty temples. But Egypt, type of the world, was earth-bound, and though eventually in the divine purpose to be linked with Israel, was to be a snare to God's people down through the ages.

Egypt's History

Before outlining the fulfilment of the prophecies, especially of Isaiah and Ezekiel concerning Egypt, it is necessary briefly to review its history. Recorded secular history commences with the ancient Egyptians, though there is considerable divergence in the dating of the thirty-one dynasties which ended with Cleopatra and the assimilation of Egypt into the Roman Empire in 31 B.C. Its first inhabitants, after the Flood, were descendants of Ham (see Psalm 105:23, 27 and Psalm 106:22) and in the Old Testament the common name for Egypt is "Mizraim" or "the land of Mizraim" (Genesis 10:6). About 800 years before Abraham visited Egypt, Menes, Egypt's first king, founded the first dynasty, and united the two kingdoms of Upper and Lower Egypt, the 750-mile tract of land, irrigated by the Nile, from 10 to 30 miles down to the Mediterranean Sea and including the Delta. It was a land which was "watered with thy foot" in contrast to Israel which drank "water of the rain of heaven" (Deuteronomy 11:10-11).

Egypt was a veritable "gift of the Nile" and with its brilliant leadership became the first great civilisation and "the granary of the world". Memphis (Noph) first, then Thebes (No-Amon), became the capitals, the former, in the Upper Kingdom, being taken by Hyksos (shepherd kings of Semitic origin) who established their dynasty at about the time that Abraham was leaving Ur. Into this period of Egypt's history moved Joseph and Moses, the exodus of Israel taking place about 1500 B.C. The God who brought Abraham from serving other gods "beyond the Euphrates" (Joshua 24:2-3) now delivered his descendants from the bondage of Pharaoh and from the idolatry of Egypt (with the "calf-worship" of Memphis) by way of the Red Sea.

Fulfilled Prophecy Concerning Egypt

"These are your gods, O Israel, who brought you up out of the land of Egypt!" was, alas, indicative of the recurrent sin of God's people, against whom His wrath waxed hot, so that He would have consumed them (see Exodus 32:1-10). But Egypt, of whom "in that day" God shall say "Blessed be Egypt My people" (Isaiah 19:25), was yet to know His righteous anger poured out on her cities and land. Isaiah prophesied against the princes of Noph (Memphis) who "caused Egypt to go astray" (Isaiah 19:13), a refrain taken up by Jeremiah (Jeremiah 46:25), by Ezekiel (Ezekiel 30:16) and by Nahum (Nahum 3:8-10).

> "Are you better than Thebes that sat by the Nile, with water around her, her rampart a sea, and water her wall? Cush was her strength; Egypt too, and that without limit; Put and the Libyans were her helpers. Yet she became an exile; she went into captivity; her infants were dashed in pieces at the head of every street; for her honored men lots were cast, and all her great men were bound in chains" (Nahum 3:8-10).

Of the fulfilment of these prophecies John Urquhart wrote, a hundred years ago, "In no land have the prophecies of the Old Testament received a more striking fulfilment than in this [Egypt]. In the misery of its people and the ruin of its cities it bears overwhelming, though involuntary, testimony to the claims of Scripture".

A visitor to the ruins of Thebes in 50 B.C. wrote, "The sun had never seen so magnificent a city" and still today the stupendous ruins of Luxor and Karnak excite the same feelings of admiration and amazement. But there was to be no extinction of the kingdom or its people, though it should be "a lowly kingdom" (Ezekiel 29:14); there should nevertheless be "no longer be a prince from the land of Egypt;" (Ezekiel 30:13). From that time to the present day there has been no native ruling prince! Today, the majority of the people as well as their rulers are Arabs, i e. Semitic in origin, only a minority of the original Mizraites, the Copts, remaining. And what of the "rivers" and "canals" of Egypt of which both Isaiah (Isaiah 19:5-8) and Ezekiel (Ezekiel 30:12) prophesied? The country's prosperity required that a third of its revenue should be expended on the maintenance of its canals, especially in the Delta area, but Herodotus records that in his day (500 B.C.) two only of the seven branches of the Delta remained open and it has yet to be seen what, in the long-term, will be the resultant effect on Egypt's economy of the vast schemes of dam construction and particularly of the closure of the Suez Canal.

Egypt's Destiny

The divine record of Egypt's glory and subsequent decay has been fulfilled to the letter, but still it remains "a lowly kingdom" (Ezekiel 29:14). Isaiah wrote of a day when there should be a "highway from Egypt to Assyria" and the Lord would bless them saying "Blessed be Egypt my people and Assyria the work of my hands, and Israel my inheritance" (Isaiah 19:23-25). Interest in developments in Western Europe, following the Treaty of Rome (1958) may have tended some students of prophecy to the view that the existing group of six nations in the European Federation were indeed six of the ten nations eventually to constitute the resuscitated Roman Empire of Daniel's prophecy. The territorial limits of this Empire we do not know, but we suggest that Egypt may be one of the kingdoms of the eastern part of the Ten Kingdom Confederacy. That the present regime in Egypt is shifting from its Communist alliance is certainly of interest, together with the evident desire to reach some sort of agreement with Israel over the alignment of territories taken over in 1967 in the Six Day War. We see in our day and generation accelerating world movements which presage for us the coming of our Lord Jesus Christ; but, sadly also for the world, the emergence of Antichrist to rule over this great Ten Kingdom Confederacy.

CHAPTER SEVEN: THE ETHIOPIANS (D.W. MILLAR)

The name "Ethiopian" comes from a Greek word meaning "burnt face" and was applied by the Greeks to dark-skinned people from the countries south and east of Egypt. There is very little known of the ancient history of these lands and a study of relations between Israel and Ethiopia in Old Testament times will get little help from contemporary history. One historian has written "We do not know the precise connotation of the Hebrew word "Cush" which the Septuagint translates into Greek as Aithiopia (Ethiopia) and many of these Scriptural references are of difficult interpretation".

Modern Ethiopia is very different from the Cush of the Old Testament. It appears that the Semitic tribes of South Arabia began to trickle over to the Horn of Africa about the days of Solomon and continued to colonize the land of Cush for many centuries, giving rise ultimately to the "Semitic-Hamitic" race which rules today over the land and over a people which is "a complex variety of ethnic elements representing a veritable mosaic of races, tribes and linguistic groups". It is necessary to mention the claim of the modern royal dynasty to be descended from the royal line of Judah, as a result of a union between the queen of Sheba and king Solomon; this claim is embodied in Article 2 of the 1955 Constitution of Ethiopia. Researchers are satisfied that this is a historic fiction, although the legend has been very strong for many centuries, being committed to writing about the 14th century A.D. in the Kebra Nagast which are regarded as the sacred writings.

Owing to Jewish migrations by way of Arabia, an early form of Judaism existed (alongside paganism) for centuries before Christ. Some of this has been carried over into the Ethiopian practice of "Christianity" today. Isaiah was given a divine charge to speak concerning Ethiopia in the days of Hezekiah. To understand the mention of Ethiopia in Isaiah's words and prophecies, it is necessary to take 2 Kings 18-20 and the whole of Isaiah 18, 20, 30 and 31 together. When the Assyrians under Sennacherib first came against Hezekiah he bought temporary respite with gold and silver taken from the house of the Lord. When Sennacherib returned, he was opposed by Egypt under the rule of an Ethiopian dynasty (see 2 Kings 19:9).

Isaiah (chapters 18 and 20) issues a divine prophecy and warning against placing any hope or expectation in the strength of Egypt and Ethiopia:

> "Then they shall be dismayed and ashamed because of Cush their hope and of Egypt their boast. And the inhabitants of this coastland will say in that day, 'Behold, this is what has happened to those in whom we hoped and to whom we fled for help to be delivered from the king of Assyria! And we, how shall we escape?'" (Isaiah 20:5-6).

Hezekiah listened to the word of God rather than the counsel of man and, because he trusted in God instead of Egypt, witnessed a great deliverance from a mighty enemy. However, as in so much prophecy, Isaiah is enabled to see beyond the immediate events and foretells a future time when Ethiopia, linked with Egypt, will submit herself to God (see Psalm 68:31; Psalm 87:4) and will revere the Lord in Zion.

At the time of the prophets, Ethiopia was closely connected with Egypt, coming under one government for some of the time and being linked with Egypt not only in the divine prophecies of judgement (Ezekiel 30), but also in the blessings to be enjoyed by the nations who will recognize the God of heaven at the time when He will enter into His earthly heritage and find joy in Israel, His inheritance. So we find Ethiopia mentioned in the great visitations of chastisement upon the nations of the earth by the Almighty, who orders the destinies of the nations and whose work of judgement is directed to the end that all nations should worship Him and recognize Israel as His people:

> "The Lord will be awesome against them; for he will famish all the gods of the earth, and to him shall bow down, each in its place, all the lands of the nations. You also, O Cushites, shall be slain by my sword. And he will stretch out his hand against the north and destroy Assyria, and he will make Nineveh a desolation, a dry waste like the desert" (Zephaniah 2:11-13).

This finds its fulfilment in Zephaniah 3, where the Lord is seen in the midst of Israel; verses 9, 10 seem to indicate that God reverses the discord of Babel and enables the dispersed peoples of the earth, including those from Ethiopia, to draw near with an offering and to serve Him in a pure language.

The sacred writings include with honour records of two individual Ethiopians: the eunuch who readily received the gospel through Philip (Acts 8), and the devotion of Ebed-melech to God's servant Jeremiah (Jeremiah 38-39). Ebed-melech was a foreigner in a very difficult situation, for the reigning king was weak and the ruling princes hated Jeremiah and the word of the Lord which he spoke, and they sought to kill him. Nevertheless Ebed-melech with great courage went to the king, and with his authority drew Jeremiah with tender care from the dungeon. It was a time of great danger, for Jerusalem was about to be destroyed and burnt. However, God's eye was not only watching over His servant Jeremiah, but was also upon Ebed-melech for good, who surely received God's promise to the stranger that has joined himself to the Lord, as recorded in Isaiah 56:3-6, which should be read in this connection.

Through the mouth of His servant Jeremiah the Lord gave to Ebed-melech one of the most remarkable personal divine assurances ever given to a Gentile (apart from the words of the Lord Jesus Himself): "I will deliver thee in that day, saith the LORD; and thou shalt not be given into the hand of the men of whom thou art afraid. For I will surely save thee ... because thou hast put thy trust in Me, saith the LORD". By his brave intervention Ebed-melech saved Jeremiah from death and influenced the history of God's people.

CHAPTER EIGHT: THE ASSYRIANS (J. RENFREW)

Origin

The Assyrian nation was of great antiquity. A reference to it is found in Genesis 10:11 in connection with Nimrod's activities, and though there appears some doubt in the text as to whether Nimrod founded that kingdom, Micah 5:6 refers to Assyria as the land of Nimrod. There is no doubt about the early civilization that was in existence in Nineveh, the capital city, which was contemporary with Ur of the Chaldees. The country was situated in the upper Mesopotamian plain, bounded on the west by the Syrian desert, on the south by Babylonia and on the north and east by the Armenian and Persian hills.

Effect on Israel

A long scriptural silence follows this early reference in Genesis until the days of the kings of Israel and Judah, when God used the Assyrian nation to chastise and afflict His people. The following kings are mentioned by name:

1. Pul, who exacted money from Menahem, king of Israel (2 Kings 15:19); probably the same person as…

2. Tiglath-pileser, who came against some of the cities of Israel and carried the captives to Assyria (2 Kings 15:29);

3. Shalmaneser, who besieged Samaria in the days of Hoshea, king of Israel, and carried Israel captive to Assyria. This same king brought men from Babylon to dwell in Samaria, where they feared the LORD and served their own gods (2 Kings 17:24);

4. Sennacherib came up against the fenced cities of Judah in the days of Hezekiah, and then later against Jerusalem. Here he met a crushing defeat at the hand of the LORD, when the angel of the LORD went forth and slew 185,000 in the camp of the Assyrians.

Some idea of Sennacherib's power can be seen in his vain boast of victory over other nations (2 Kings 19:12-13), but he reckoned without the God of Israel. Hezekiah's prayer and the reply he received from the LORD are a remarkable demonstration of the power of prayer and the LORD's intervention on the behalf of His people. Sennacherib returned to his own land greatly humiliated, later to meet an untimely death at the hands of his sons (Isaiah 37-38).

Prophetical References

As mentioned earlier, the Assyrian nation was an instrument in the hand of the LORD for the chastisement of His people. Through Isaiah (Isaiah 7:7,20) Ahaz was warned of punishment because of his sins and provocation of the LORD (2 Chronicles 28:25). In Isaiah 10:5 the LORD refers to the Assyrian as "the rod of my anger; the staff in their hands is my fury!" He also reveals that the Assyrian king was unaware of this, and when the LORD had accomplished His purposes He would then punish the king of Assyria for his pride. Further, the LORD would stir up a scourge against the king of Assyria and his yoke would be broken (Isaiah 10:26-27). Then finally, when the Shoot came forth from the stock of Jesse, the LORD would set His hand to recover the remnant of His people from Assyria and elsewhere (Isaiah 11:1,11).

In the glorious days of the reign the Prince of peace, Assyria, together with Israel and Egypt, would be a blessing in the midst of the earth (Isaiah 19:24). Micah also refers to Israel's deliverance from the bondage of the Assyrian, when the Ruler of Israel would be manifested, and the land of Assyria would be laid waste with the sword (Micah 5:2,6). It is remarkable how two of the minor prophets, Jonah and

Nahum, devote the whole of their written prophecies to Nineveh. Consideration has already been given to the LORD's mercy towards that great city and the impact of Jonah's message upon the king and inhabitants of the city. It is obvious that the LORD had a particular purpose in sending Jonah there.

Was it to remind them of the sovereignty of the God of Israel? The message had its due effect and led to some correction of the violence and the evil that were practiced in the city. Nahum (3:1-4) reveals more of the conditions prevalent in the city (though possibly at a later date) - lies, plunder, rumbling wheels, galloping horses and bounding chariots, in short a nation drunken with power and military victory; upon such a nation God was about

to stretch forth His hand in judgement and Nineveh would be destroyed. What was once a populous city would become a desolation and the inhabitants scattered upon the mountains with none to gather them (Nahum 3:18). Zephaniah also refers to this in his prophecy. The joyous city would become the habitation of beasts, and a lodging place of the pelican and porcupine (Zephaniah 2:13-15). This scripture has been literally fulfilled, and the modern name of the city is "Tell Kuyun-jik" which means "mound of many sheep".

Jeremiah refers to the punishment of the king of Assyria (Jeremiah 50:18). History records that a combined force of Medes, Babylonians and Scythians laid seige to Nineveh which fell as a result of breaches in the defences made by flooding rivers. Thus was fulfilled the word of the LORD through His servants the prophets.

CHAPTER NINE: THE SYRIANS (DAVID JONES)

Syria is the Revised Version term for Aram or the country of the Arameans, the descendants of Aram, son of Shem (Genesis 10:22). It lies to the north-east of Israel. Besides the Arameans proper, peoples from various Semitic tribes settled in Aram, such as Terah's family in Paddan-aram. So Laban and even Jacob are referred to as Syrians or Arameans (Genesis 31:24; Deuteronomy 26:5 and RV margin).

Damascus was well-known in Abraham's time (Genesis 14:15,15:2), and later became the Syrian capital. Partly because of continual immigration, the peoples of Syria were never a fully united nation until after the Old Testament history closed. At various periods, however, local leaders attracted sufficient support to influence and make raids on the surrounding countries (e.g. Judges 3:8-10, RV margin). In later years, several local concentrations of power developed in Syria, and with these Saul and David had to contend (1 Samuel 14:47; 2 Samuel 8:3-9, 2 Samuel 10:6-19). Towards the end of his reign Solomon had trouble with Rezon, who achieved power in Damascus (1 Kings 11:23-25). From then on, in the history of 1 and 2 Kings, we find Syria engaged in constant warring against Israel and Judah (1 Kings 22:1; 2 Kings 6:8) or in alliance with Israel against Judah (1 Kings 15:19; 2 Kings 16:5-6).

The last of these alliances was the memorable confederacy of Isaiah 7:2 between Rezin and Pekah. That ended, as Isaiah foretold, in the subjugation of Damascus by the Assyrians (2 Kings 16:9). The Syrians continued subject till the downfall of the Assyrian Empire, when they easily fell before the power of Nebuchadnezzar. Being so close together geographically, Israel, Judah and Syria would naturally have become involved in each other's affairs. The Scriptures show however, that in

God's general supervision of these nations, many of their initiatives for or against each other were prompted by Him (e.g. 1 Kings 11:23-25; 2 Kings 10:32, 13:3, 15:37). It is impossible for us to weigh the counsels of the Most High in such matters. The outcome of a particular battle did not always indicate God's approval of the ways of the victorious nation. And although the Lord may have used a certain nation to chastise His people, that did not give it licence to perpetrate atrocities on His people; for these they themselves would be chastised.

The Old Testament teems with references to Syria, and space forbids us to mention even all the main portions. We wish to comment on some of the prophetic statements about Syria, especially in her relations with Israel and Judah, briefly placing them in historical context, but making no claim that the statements are presented in strict chronological order.

1. Unknown Prophet speaking to Ahab (1 Kings 20:28-42)

The Syrian's contempt of God as a God of the hills but not of the valleys brought swift judgement. The Lord seems to have regarded certain battles as part of a general education about Himself to the Syrians and to Israel. On this occasion the Lord was instructing them in a language they understood! Ahab did not take seriously the task of executing God's judgement on Ben-hadad, and he let Ben-hadad live when it was in his power to kill him (1 Kings 20:33-34). This bears comparison with king Saul's attitude in sparing Agag's life (1 Samuel 15:8, 20). We learn the awesome responsibility laid on leaders under God, and the penalty exacted of them when they lead the people astray. Ahab lost his life under this prophecy from the arrow shot "at random" in a further battle against Ben-hadad, this time with king Jehoshaphat of Judah on Israel's side (1 Kings 22:34-38).

2. Prophecies through Elisha

(a) "Therefore the leprosy of Naaman shall cling to you" (2 Kings 5:27). Elisha's dealings with Naaman in 2 Kings 5 may be thought of as an outreach in grace to Syria. Elisha fervently strove to impress on Naaman that God alone could and did cure him, and Gehazi's action in asking gifts of Naaman threatened to cloud Elisha's clear witness; hence this prophecy. However, an unmistakeable beam shone to Syria from God's faithful servant in most unfavourable circumstances, when Israel was low spiritually and she and Syria were at loggerheads. Our Lord's words about Naaman the Syrian are pertinent (Luke 4:27).

(b) 2 Kings 6:8-23 presents two further features through which God appealed to Syria:

(i) Elisha was able to give to the king of Israel warnings about Ben-hadad's plans;

(ii) kindness was shown to the captured Syrian army because of Elisha's advice. As a result, the Syrian raidings ceased, but not for long.

(c) "Tomorrow about this time a seah of fine flower shall be sold for a shekel, and two seahs of barley for a shekel, at the gate of Samaria" (2 Kings 7:1). A lengthy siege by Syria had reduced Samaria, Israel's capital, to dire straits. God intervened in the remarkable events of 2 Kings 7; the Syrian army was caused to hear "the noise of a great host" (verse 6) and fled in fear, leaving their camp full of provisions, as God had said through Elisha. In these events God chastened both Israel and Syria, and used them to speak to His people through the prophet. Probably there were individuals who responded, but the nation as a whole became hardened. At least in Syria Elisha was gaining respect (2 Kings 8:7-44).

(d) "Go, say to him (Ben-hadad), 'You shall certainly recover,' but the Lord has shown me that he shall certainly die … you are to be king over Syria" (2 Kings 8:10,13). Elisha wept before Hazael as he thought of all the evil and distress Hazael would bring to Israel. Hazael was a wicked man, yet God was appointing him king of Syria (see also 1 Kings 19:15,17) to be the executor of His judgements on His people. This was history in the making.

(e) To Joash of Israel: "You should have struck five or six times; then you would have struck down Syria until you had made an end of it, but now you will strike down Syria only three times" (2 Kings 13:19). Joash's response to Elisha's death-bed request was half-hearted, and the prophet's final blessing on the king was only appropriate. For the fulfilment see verse 25.

3. Jonah

Jonah prophesied that Israel's border would be restored from the entering in of Hamath unto the sea of the Arabah (2 Kings 14:25). Hamath was many miles north of Damascus, so this prophetic statement implied the occupation of Syrian territory, which took place under Jeroboam II of Israel (2 Kings 14. 24-28). Not since the days of David and Solomon had Damascus and Syria been subject to Israel to this extent.

4. Amos

> "For three transgressions of Damascus, and for four, I will not revoke the punishment, because they have threshed Gilead with threshing sledges of iron. So I will send a fire upon the house of Hazael, and it shall devour the strongholds of Ben-hadad. I will break the gate-bar of Damascus, and cut off the inhabitants from the Valley of Aven, and him who holds the scepter from Beth-eden; and the people of Syria shall go into exile to Kir," says the Lord" (Amos 1:3-5).

THE NATIONS OF THE OLD TESTAMENT 57

This prophecy seems to refer to the barbarous military enterprises of Hazael and his son Ben-hadad. 2 Kings 10:32-33 records that Hazael attacked Gilead, and Elisha foretold Hazael's barbarity. Such atrocities called for decisive judgement on Syria. Not all the military campaigns against Syria are recorded in Scripture, so it may not be possible to identify in Scripture all the features of Amos's prophecy about God's judgements on Syria; but the final statement of Amos 1:5 seems to refer to the Assyrian destruction of Damascus and the taking of its people to Kir (2 Kings 16:9). This prophecy was given at least twenty years before its fulfilment, probably much longer.

5. Isaiah

(a) Isaiah 7:4-9, 14:46, 8:5-7. The armies of Israel and Syria, under kings Pekah and Rezin, were besieging Jerusalem (Isaiah 7:1; 2 Kings 16:5). Ahaz king of Judah was greatly perturbed, and Isaiah was sent by God to reassure him that Israel and Syria would not be allowed to gain their objective, which was to set up their own, king in place of Ahaz. Ahaz asked and paid for help from the king of Assyria against Israel and Syria (2 Kings 16:7-9), and received it, resulting in the very destruction of Damascus which Isaiah had foretold to Ahaz (Isaiah 7:16, 8:6-7). A detailed sequence of events here is difficult to determine. 2 Chronicles 28:5-6 indicates that the Israelite and Syrian armies did much damage to the kingdom of Judah, but Jerusalem was not overcome. Even at this late hour, prior to their own destruction, the Syrians were still being used by God to bring home to Judah and Ahaz the seriousness of their idolatrous practices (2 Chronicles 28:1-6).

Isaiah 7:8 gives a further 65 years before Israel (Ephraim) would be finally broken as a nation, although Samaria was to be sacked fairly soon. The same can probably be said of Syria and Damascus. Though

Damascus and other principal cities, (see Isaiah 10:9) were spoiled soon after the Isa. 7 prophecy, a residual power to raise armies was yet to be dealt with by God, as later prophecies outline.

(b) Isaiah 17:1-3. "Behold, Damascus will cease to be a city and will become a heap of ruins ..." So at last the final destruction of Damascus is foretold. Already, as Isaiah wrote, Damascus was no longer to be regarded as a city, but soon it would be a heap of rubble. That the Syrian kingdom would cease probably means that the residue of the population allowed to remain in Syria would become subject to the occupying power, Assyria.

6. Jeremiah

"Hamath and Arpad are confounded, for they have heard bad news; they melt in fear,... Damascus has become feeble ... And I will kindle a fire in the wall of Damascus, and it shall devour the strongholds of Ben-hadad" (Jeremiah 49:23-27). This possibly refers to the state of mind of, and what was done to, the Syrian populace on the advent of Nebuchadnezzar's troops to subjugate this part of the Assyrian Empire to Babylonian domination.

7. Ezekiel

There are minor references to Syria in Ezekiel 16:57 and 27:16-18. But the references in 47:16-18 and 48:1 to Damascus and other Syrian cities relate to the dividing up of the land of Israel at the beginning of the Millennium. Note the mention of Hamath, which was given as the northern extremity of the territory designated for Israelite use by God through Moses (Numbers 34:8). As Hamath was well to the north of Damascus, this implied that a large part of Syrian territory was originally included in the Promised Land. Also in God's promise to Abraham, the northern boundary of the land was given as the river Euphrates (Genesis 15:18).

As mentioned earlier, the inclusion of much of Syria within the actual borders of Israel was only attained for brief periods, during the reigns of Solomon and Jeroboam II of Israel. Ezekiel's prophecy shows, however, that this will be a permanent feature of Israeli territory during the Millennium.

CHAPTER TEN: THE BABYLONIANS (LAURIE BURROWS AND PETER HICKLING)

The city of Babylon was founded, as Babel, by Nimrod, according to Genesis 10:10. It was subsequently destroyed or sacked several times, and was subject to the dominance, first of Ur, then of the Assyrians. Babylon repeatedly struggled for its independence, rebelling against the various governors appointed by the Assyrian power. Sargon II of Assyria sacked the city, deporting some of the chief rebels to Samaria, but there was another revolt against Sennacherib in 689 B.C., despite these measures. Sennacherib's grandson Samas-sum-ukin was later appointed governor of the city, but he quarrelled with his brother Ashurbanipal of Assyria, and in the subsequent war Babylon was damaged by fire. At length the decline of the Assyrian empire enabled Nabopolassar, a Chaldean, to assert Babylonian independence, and occupy the throne in 626 B.C. Nabopolassar drove back the Assyrians, capturing Nineveh in 612 B.C.

His son, Nebuchadnezzar, gained a decisive victory over the Egyptians at the battle of Carchemish in 605 B.C. In the same year he carried off hostages from Judah, inducting Daniel, to Babylon. Judah rebelled against its Babylonian overlords, despite warnings by the prophet Jeremiah, and in 597 B.C. Nebuchadnezzar besieged and took Jerusalem, carrying away Jehoiachin (2 Kings 24:10-17). Zedekiah, appointed as a puppet king by Nebuchadnezzar, also rebelled; Jerusalem was again besieged, and Zedekiah was taken captive to Babylon (2 Kings 24:20-25, 27). Jerusalem was eventually destroyed by the Babylonians in 587 B.C., and its citizens further deported to Babylon (2 Kings 25:8-21).

THE NATIONS OF THE OLD TESTAMENT 61

Under Nebuchadnezzar Babylon was at the zenith of its power, and it is against this background of apparently secure dominion that the prophecies of Babylon's downfall should be examined.

Prophecies

Three Old Testament prophets prophesied against Babylon: Isaiah, Jeremiah and Daniel. Of these, Daniel's prophecies of the fall of Babylon were in response to the requests of Nebuchadnezzar and Belshazzar for interpretations of visions, and were not so detailed as those of Isaiah and Jeremiah. The three prophecies are reviewed below:

(a) Isaiah

Isaiah's ministry extended from the end of Uzziah's reign at least until Hezekiah's reign, and probably into the reign of Manasseh, although he apparently played no public part in this last reign. Even at the end of his life, the fall of Jerusalem was more than 100 years in the future, and the fall of Babylon over 150 years away. This gap in time makes his prophecies the more remarkable, since they contain specific and accurate allusions to persons and nations, and in places read as though the events referred to had actually occurred.

There are two principal passages dealing with Babylon: Isaiah 13:1 to 14:23 and 44:24-45:7, The first reveals God's intention to bring the Medes against Babylon (Isaiah 13:17). God reveals Himself as Lord of the nations, able to use Gentile armies to fulfil His purpose, for they are referred to as "My consecrated ones" (Isaiah 13:3). The passage lays special emphasis on the pride of the Babylonians and contrasts the splendour of the city with the desolation to which it will ultimately be reduced. "It will never be inhabited or lived in for all generations; no Arab will pitch his tent there; no shepherds will make their flocks lie down there. But wild animals will lie down there" (Isaiah 13:20-21). It should be noted that the passage presents Babylon as the oppressor who has taken Israel captive (Isaiah 14:1-2).

Chapters 44 and 45 seem to present the situation near the end of the exile, when God has raised up one who is to break the power of Babylon. This one is revealed in Isaiah 44:28 to be Cyrus, whom God has called by name, although Cyrus himself was not yet born.

(b) Jeremiah

Jeremiah wrote his prophecy against Babylon in the fourth year of Zedekiah's reign (Jeremiah 51:59-60). The idols of Babylon, Bel and Merodach, could not save her from the nation which the Lord would bring from the north against her (Jeremiah 50:2-3,9). Prosperous Babylon would become a wilderness and a desert because she had plundered Jerusalem, the Lord's heritage (Jeremiah 50:11-12). The land which irrigation made fertile would be dried up, and not inhabited from generation to generation (Jeremiah 50:38-39). The Medes are again given as God's instrument in the destruction of Babylon (Jeremiah 51:11).

(c) Daniel

Daniel, in interpreting the dream of Nebuchadnezzar, told him that his kingdom would be overthrown and replaced by another. This happened in the regency of Belshazzar, the grandson of Nebuchadnezzar, when Daniel, interpreting the writing on the wall, prophesied the immediate downfall of the kingdom (Daniel 5).

Prophecy Fulfilled

Events occurred just as the prophets had foretold. Cyrus, the ruler of the kingdom of Anshan, took over the province of Persia. By 550 B.C. he defeated Astyages, king of Media, and himself became king of the

Medes. He conquered Croesus and his kingdom of Lydia, and in 549 B.C. marched through Assyria. In 539 B.C. his armies entered Babylon, having by a considerable feat of civil engineering diverted the flow of the Euphrates, enabling troops to enter the city along the river bed (see Isaiah 44:27). The surprise was complete; the city fell literally in a day, as it had been predicted. Cyrus permitted the captives to return to their native land, but did not himself destroy Babylon. Xerxes destroyed the city in 478 B.C., and although Alexander planned to restore it, he met his death there before the work progressed far.

The city fell completely into ruins, until all that was left when archaeologists began to investigate the site was a number of ruined mounds. The Euphrates has changed its course, flowing some distance from the ruins. No one now lives in the dry and desolate area; the little Arab settlement of Babil preserves the name, but lies some miles to the north. Fallen is Babylon the Great - according to the word of the Lord.

Babylon: Prediction of End-Time Aspects

The Old Testament prophets had a good deal to say about Babylon and its kings, which is only to be expected having in mind the city's importance to Israel over a long period, but these prophecies also have in view parallel events future to our day, and it is not always obvious which period is being dealt with. Perhaps there is a tendency to assume that Isaiah and Jeremiah, in giving the Lord's message to their contemporaries, would naturally refer to present or imminent events, but is that necessarily so? There are a number of considerations suggesting that the important prophecies in Isaiah 13:1-14:25 and Jeremiah 50:1-51:64 contain direct references to a Babylon yet to be built which will be associated with the momentous world events preceding the coming of the Son of Man.

That the rebuilding will take place on the original site seems to follow from the intimate lending of prophetic allusions to both phases of the city's history. Now consider such statements in Isaiah as:

> "The day of the Lord comes, cruel, with wrath and fierce anger, to make the land a desolation" (Isaiah 13:9).

> "the sun will be dark at its rising, and the moon will not shed its light" (Isaiah 13:10).

> "I will punish the world for its evil" (Isaiah 13:11).

> "I will make people more rare than fine gold" (Isaiah 13:12)

> "The day of his fierce anger" (Isaiah 13:13).

These and many similar ones, although couched in poetic language, can only be understood to describe events far greater than those attending any of the assaults made upon Babylon from the time of Isaiah until it disappeared from the page of history. Again, the astronomical and terrestrial catastrophes described in Isaiah 13:10-13 point strongly to pre-millennial days (Matthew 24:29-30). Isaiah 13:17 seems at first sight to be a clear reference to the taking of Babylon by Darius the Mede in Daniel's day (Daniel 5:30-31). But the following verses describe an overthrow like that of Sodom and Gomorrah; the use of such a comparison implies that Babylon was to be quickly and completely destroyed, never to rise again, a prediction which has so far had no fulfilment either in Biblical or secular history.

When Darius "received the kingdom" (Daniel 5:31) Babylon was not destroyed. History records that the army of Cyrus entered the city by stealth; Scripture testifies that it was still a city of some importance in the days of Ezra (Ezra 7:9) and it is likely that the same place is referred to even in the New Testament by Peter (1 Peter 5:15). It is said that Alexander the Great once entered the city but thereafter it suffered a gradual decline. Clearly Babylon has not yet experienced sudden destruction, so that much of Isaiah 13 and 14 must have a future application.

Did Joshua and Zerubbabel and their friends, lately emancipated from Babylon's oppression, say, "How you are fallen from heaven, O Day Star, son of Dawn!...You said in your heart, 'I will ascend to heaven; above the stars of God I will set my throne on high; I will sit on the mount of assembly" (Isaiah 14:12-13)? It is submitted that the "rest from your pain" (verse 3) must have a more important application than to that faithful remnant, for Nebuchadnezzar's pride, although great, was limited to the earthly sphere (Daniel 4:30). The king described in Isaiah 14:13-14 is more satisfactorily identified with the king of the north (Daniel 11:36) who will dominate all the nations in the last days and will even aspire to the position of deity.

When Seraiah gathered the exiled Jews around him in Babylon and read Jeremiah's message (Jeremiah 50, 51) no doubt they were encouraged and reassured by the prophecy that Babylon would soon be punished for her wickedness. Their sad spirits would be revived as they were reminded of the Lord's care for them (Jeremiah 50:19,34; 51:24, 28). As in the Isaiah oracle, however, Jeremiah's message has running through it the theme of complete and sudden destruction (Jeremiah 50:13; 51:29). Sodom and Gomorrah are again used illustratively (Jeremiah 50:39-40). Babylon's crisis is to have world-wide repercussions (Jeremiah 50:46). So Israel's two great prophets jointly witness to the revival to unprecedented power of the city of Babylon, only to be destroyed for ever under divine judgement for its wickedness.

That these two prophets have to do with events yet to come is further confirmed by their similarity to the undoubtedly end-time New Testament Revelation (Revelation 17:18). For instance, Revelation mentions "the great prostitute who is seated on many waters" (Revelation 17:1) and identifies the harlot with "Babylon the great' (Revelation 17:5) and Jeremiah describes Babylon as dwelling upon many waters (Jeremiah 51:13). In both books the end of the city is likened to a stone sinking in water (Jeremiah 51:63-64; Revelation 18:21). Whereas John says, "Fallen, fallen is Babylon the great" (Revelation 14:8, 18:2), Isaiah says, "fallen, fallen is Babylon" (Isaiah 21:9) and Jeremiah says, "Suddenly Babylon has fallen" (Jeremiah 51:8). Old and New Testaments agree that heaven will rejoice over Babylon (Revelation 18:20; Jeremiah 51:48) and they both record the Lord's call to His people to escape from Babylon's evil influence and impending doom (Jeremiah 51:6, 45; Revelation 18:4).

This short study shows the threefold emphasis placed by Scripture upon Babylon's wickedness and its consequences. The satanically inspired alliance of commerce and false religion centred in the revived city of Babylon will sink under its final catastrophe, never to rise again. Men of all ages are thus warned of the extreme spiritual danger of succumbing to the attractions of an ungodly world. "Come out of her, my people, lest you take part in her sins, lest you share in her plagues;" (Revelation 18:4).

CHAPTER ELEVEN: THE MEDO-PERSIANS (PETER HICKLING)

Before the nation of Israel had come into existence, God promised to Abraham that his posterity would become a great people, and to that people God gave the land of Canaan, for "an everlasting possession" (Genesis 17:5-8). God revealed that, in the fulfilment of His purposes on earth, what was to become the nation of Israel had a special place. As the development of this purpose proceeded, God redeemed Israel from Egypt, and at Sinai the people agreed to be bound by the provisions of the conditional covenant which God offered to them (Exodus 19 and 24). This covenant promised the presence of God among the people, so that He could display His glory through them, but it also brought severe penalties for disobedience.

Privilege involved responsibility, and if the covenant were broken, it would bring forth the vengeance of the covenant (Leviticus 26:25); God could not dwell in peace among a rebellious people. Moses prophesied just before his death, when the people were about to enter the promised land, that they would forsake the God that made them (Deuteronomy 32:25), and so it proved. Israel had not been long in the land before Canaanite practices were adopted, and a long series of prophets sent by God warned of the vengeance of the covenant, with varying response. Among the last of these was Jeremiah, who revealed God's intention of delivering Judah (the northern kingdom of Israel had fallen previously) into the hands of Nebuchadnezzar (Jeremiah 21). God's longsuffering had finally come to an end, and the nation was to be taken from the Land - but only for a period.

Nebuchadnezzar appeared, conquered, and took the people captive to his capital, Babylon, and this captivity was to continue for seventy years (Jeremiah 25:12). The might of Chaldea seemed invincible, but

God had prepared an instrument for the deliverance of the captives in Cyrus, king of Persia and Media (Isaiah 44:28). The early history of Cyrus is obscure, but Herodotus records that he was the son of Mandane, daughter of Astyages, king of the Medes. His father was Cambyses, king of Persia, who ruled from Anshan.

On the death of Cambyses, Cyrus became king, and in 550 B.C. he defeated Astvages, and became himself "king of the Medes", the title used of him by the Babylonian Nabonidus. Next he defeated Croesus, king of Lydia, then turned the path of his conquests east, towards north-west India. Finally he turned south to Babylon. In 539 B.C. the Persian armies entered Babylon on the dried-up bed of the diverted river. Belshazzar was slain (Daniel 5:30); the Chaldean empire finally fell, and Cyrus became the undisputed overlord of an empire extending from India to the Mediterranean.

In the first year of Cyrus as ruler over this great empire, he fulfilled the purpose for which God had given him this power, in making the proclamation giving the Jews the liberty to return to Jerusalem with his blessing, to build a house for the God of Israel (Ezra 1:3). Cyrus himself did not fully appreciate the character of Jehovah as the only true God, since he also caused the worship of the Babylonian god Marduk to be carried on, and he seems to have had the general policy of encouraging the worship of national gods by the peoples concerned. Nonetheless, as far as God's people were concerned, he was the instrument God used to give them their liberty. God's desire and purpose was that His people should dwell in the land which He had given them, and that He should dwell in the midst of them in the House on which He had put His name.

At first the returned exiles were eager to prosecute the work; they ordered materials, using the grant which Cyrus had given them (Ezra 3:7), and began the work with joy. Soon the local inhabitants, colonists

THE NATIONS OF THE OLD TESTAMENT 69

imported by the Assyrians, wanted - probably not very sincerely - to help in the work. They were not the Lord's people; they stood in no covenant relationship to Him, and their offer could not be accepted, but its rejection was the pretext for opposition which brought the work to a halt. The work was then neglected for some sixteen years, until the vigorous exhortation of Haggai and Zechariah moved the people, under Zerubbabel, to recommence it. The civil servants who governed the area required to know whether permission had been given for this building, and on being told of the decree of Cyrus, wrote to their head office asking for the files in Babylon to be checked to see whether such a decree had been issued.

The record was eventually found in Ecbatana, the capital of Media, and king Darius confirmed the decree of Cyrus, and himself reinforced it by providing that offerings should be made available for sacrifice (Ezra 6:9). Once more God used the resources of a Gentile king in furthering His purposes through Israel, and the House was finished and dedicated with this aid (Ezra 6:15-17). The rebuilding of the House of God had received official support, and Artaxerxes, in his turn, encouraged the service of the House of God, and sent Ezra in 458 B.C. to administer it (Ezra 7:12-26).

As Cyrus and Darius had done before him, he made generous grants for the purchase of sacrifices, and he also exempted the priests and servants of the House of God from taxation. Ezra 7:27 reveals that God had put this into the king's heart; there must have been some receptiveness towards God - even faith towards Him - in the heart of this Gentile king. Thirteen years later, in 445 B.C., Nehemiah heard of the broken-down state of the walls of Jerusalem and the low morale of the people (Nehemiah 1), and he resolved to ask Artaxerxes for leave to go to Jerusalem to promote the rebuilding of the city. Once more God used the royal power of Persia to further His purpose. Nehemiah was permitted to go to Jerusalem and begin the rebuilding of the walls.

Against the initial scorn, and the continued opposition of Sanballat (later governor of Samaria) and others whose interests were affected by the fortification of the city, the walls were eventually finished, and Nehemiah was able to enforce proper rule and the observance of God's law. At this point the Biblical record ceases, and the Medo-Persian rulers cease to be used directly as instruments of God's purpose. In 331 B.C. their empire was overthrown by Alexander the Great; yet God's purpose in the Jews continued, culminating in His sending His Son. "God chose the weak things of the world, that He might put to shame the things that are strong" (1 Corinthians 1:27).

CHAPTER TWELVE: THE GIBEONITES (DR. A.T. DOODSON)

Undoubtedly one of the finest and most stirring themes in the Scriptures is the provision for the blessing which God purposed upon the Gentiles, those who had no share in the covenants of promise, and were without hope. We who are Gentiles by descent eagerly search the Scriptures for evidences of God's care for the strangers to the covenants, though we see in the covenants themselves God's intention that in Abraham and in Isaac and in Jacob all the earth should in due course be blessed. There were some, though, who did not have to wait the fulfilment of God's ultimate purposes, but who were enabled by His grace to become partakers with His chosen people in such blessings, privileges, and responsibilities as were then made known to men.

We see something of this in Deuteronomy 23:3-8 in the commandments concerning the Ammonite and the Moabite in the one category, and the Edomite and the Egyptian in the other. The Assembly of the LORD was indeed closely guarded, but in a certain measure the heart of God responded to the work of faith, whether in Abraham or in the hearts of some poor strangers who desired to be with the people of God, who looked on the sojourning people as strangers in the world, and deemed it to be a far better thing for themselves to be strangers to the world than to be strangers to God.

No doubt it was a hard thing to know that many generations must pass ere the full liberty of the chosen people could be shared by the strangers, but this test of faith is itself akin to that of Abraham, who had to look down the ages to see the fulness of the blessing come to his descendants. It is worthy of note that in many of these things men are taught to esteem the blessings to come to their posterity, for parents to save up for the children (2 Corinthians 12:14) in a very special and blessed way. Indeed we have to take a wide view of many of the parables of the Scriptures, in which we have to consider the ways of God through- generation after generation, to see the characteristics of the parents in the sons, and to note how God speaks to peoples as though He were speaking to their long-dead progenitors.

Even concerning men of whom it was written, "You shall not seek their peace or their prosperity all your days forever" (Deuteronomy 23:6), hope is not entirely cut off, though ten generations (verse 3) must await the full blessing. What a fine distinction is made in these words! It is not that men of this class are to be persuaded to come in, but rather is it that the seeker after the God of Israel is not debarred so long as he values the hope and is prepared with patience to wait for it. Then Edom the "brother" (verse 8) and the Egyptian are placed upon the same footing, and in their lifetime may hope to see their descendants of the third generation occupying the place of privilege. A distinction may be drawn between the people of Egypt and the Pharaohs of Egypt, analogous to that which we know exists between the people of this world and the rulers of this world-darkness. God loved the world, and this is again borne out from Isaiah 19:24-25:

> "In that day Israel will be the third with Egypt and with Assyria, a blessing in the midst of the earth: for that the Lord of Hosts has blessed them, saying, Blessed be Egypt my people, and Assyria the work of my hands, and Israel my inheritance."

The cases of Rahab and Ruth are well known, and we shall not deal with them in detail, save to remark that entrance into the blessings of Israel was in all probability conferred in a very special way through their husbands, a type of the ease with which the Church which is the Body receives blessing through the heavenly Bridegroom. It is our hope to set forth some reflections upon the dealings of God with certain peoples, and with the above introductions we shall now turn our attention to the history of the Gibeonites. Please read Joshua 9. It is generally remarked concerning the Book of Joshua that it should be read in connection with the Epistle to the Ephesians, for each deals with a place of inheritance and blessing, and each deals with accompanying warfare.

The glorious entry into the Land of Canaan and the victory over Jericho were followed by the defeat at Ai, and the people had to learn the lesson that it is often in the flush of victory that we have need to beware of the power of the Adversary, who takes advantage of our pride in our victory to tempt us to go on in our own strength. Even after Ai, where the final victory was assured by the advice and help of God, one feels that Joshua and his fellows had not fully learnt the lesson to do all things solely by the counsel of God.

The "schemes of the Devil" are made manifest very early. His first move is often associated with intimidation, whether in the case of Pharaoh in Egypt, or in that of the Council in Jerusalem who beat the apostles and commanded them not to teach the things of the Lord. So we read of a great confederation of kings to fight against Israel, and then of the Gibeonites who worked "with cunning" and sought an alliance with Israel They went to work very thoroughly, every detail had been planned so that Joshua would not suspect them to be inhabitants of the land. So they professed to come from a far country and they were so wily that they only spoke of that which bad been done in Egypt and beyond Jordan. There was no word of sharing in the Land of Promise. Moreover, even as the Devil is apt to quote Scripture, so these men were ostensibly covered by the law of Deuteronomy 20-11 and 15, and they offered themselves as servants.

In that Joshua and the Princes of Israel sought not the counsel of God, they made a covenant with these people, and it was not until later that the people found out the true state of affairs and murmured against the Princes. A dlfficult problem has indeed to be solved: how shall the Gibeonites be treated? Shall they be put to the sword? Not so, for the Princes had sworn unto them by the LORD, the God of Israel. Well then, let them live, some might have said, but let them be banished to the far corners of the Land. Again, not so, but, said Joshua, let them be servants indeed, hewers of wood and drawers of water for the congregation, and for the altar of the LORD.

Mere human wisdom would stand aghast at such a decision. Should such a people be allowed even to touch anything that was to be used in the LORD's service? Here indeed we have an insight into the perfect wisdom of God, for if the people of Gibeon had simply been made to be slaves, then the temptation would have been strong to have made many more slaves. Even so, the people of Israel did not escape the snare of Satan, for we afterwards read how they did not slay all the inhabitants of the land, for "Now when the people of Israel grew strong, they put the Canaanites to forced labor" (Joshua 17:13), and in due course they learnt the truth of Deuteronomy 20:18, for their slaves taught them the abominations of the Canaanites.

But they did not learn any of these things from the Gibeonites, who seemed to have had a quiet resting place among the Israelites for many centuries, and God severely punished the people of Israel for the transgression of that ultra-righteous man Saul, who put some of the Gibeonites to death, "so that we should have no place in all the territory of Israel" (see 2 Samuel 21). God had a care for them, for the Princes of Israel had sworn to them in the Name of the LORD. Moreover, when the men who had deceived Joshua were confronted with the deception, their confession (Joshua 9:24) must have had some weight:

"it was told to your servants for a certainty that the LORD your God had commanded ... to give you all the land ... And now, behold, we are in your hand. Whatever seems good and right in your sight to do to us, do it."

They no longer held out for the letter of the covenant made with them. And it seemed good and right unto the LORD to make them hewers of wood and drawers of water ... for the altar of the LORD. This was the secret of their being kept from being a snare unto Israel. Where men would no doubt have kept them from the altar, God gave them some work to do, however humble it might be, in service for Him. As the Gibeonites hewed that wood, their minds would in some degree or other be taken up with the use of that fuel in maintaining the fire on the altar, and we may seek to impress upon each and all that God has a care for those who are taken up with the service of the altar and that they will neither be stumbled nor will stumble others if they are kept very near to the God of the Altar, in the place which He chooses (verse 27).

This is a lesson drawn from a people in a humble condition, doing humble service, but in these days the strangers to the covenants who are made near in Christ have reserved for them in this life a place of service, the highest blessing we may enjoy on earth, in the House of God on earth today if they have humility to come to the Place of the Name and own themselves to be bondservants of the Lord.

CHAPTER THIRTEEN: THE RECHABITES (DR. A.T. DOODSON)

The purposes of God in His dealings with aliens, as was said in the last chapter, are of very great interest to us who have known what it means to be strangers and aliens. The history of the Rechabites is of particular interest, because the purposes of God in them are not revealed until after many centuries have rolled their course. We shall seek to show that the events of Jeremiah 35 give the consummation of God's purposes, as first announced in some measure in the days of Moses. One lifetime does not suffice for the deep counsels of God to be fully worked out, as we see in connection with the promises to Abraham, and the spiritual experiences we pass through in our lifetime are often only fully exemplified by the experiences of a nation as revealed in the Scriptures.

It is highly significant that a nation is oft-times spoken to by God as though He were addressing their ancestor. Thus the nation of Israel is addressed as though Jacob the man is being spoken to, the characteristics of his sons are seen in the after-history of their descendants, while the promises given to the former are taken as received by them, though the actual fulfilment is experienced by their children. With this preamble, please read the chapter of Jeremiah and note the prominence given to Jehonadab. The reward given for the behaviour of the Rechabites in carrying out the commands of Jehonadab is attributed to the man long dead. This remarkable man appears for the first time in 2 Kings 10:15-31.

The day of judgement on the wicked house of Ahab has arrived, and the anointed man Jehu has been made the instrument of God's vengeance. In verse 15 we read that in the course of his work Jehu "met Jehonadab the son of Rechab coming to meet him." The great king stops his chariot that he might be assured of the fellowship of the great commoner, and it is for us to examine as to which of these men is really the greater. There can be no doubt at all that Jehonadab was a great man for he was closely associated with Jehu in the judgements on the worshippers of Baal.

Moreover, it is clear that as he was coming to meet Jehu then he must have had some fellowship with Elisha, who had anointed Jehu for this great work of God. It is indeed strange that this man, regarded as next to the king in importance, should so suddenly appear in the picture, stranger still that he should so suddenly disappear from the picture after the events of this chapter. He appears again, so to speak, only at the reading of his last will and testament as declared by the Rechabites to Jeremiah.

As we seek to trace the history of Jehonadab we quickly realize that he was not an Israelite by descent, but a Kenite (1 Chronicles 2:55). The Kenites appear in the pages of Scripture from time to time. They were among the friends of David to whom he sent portions from the spoil of Ziglag, just before he came to the throne (1 Samuel 30:29), a fact which speaks well for them. They received very special consideration from Saul on that notable day when he went to fight against the Amalekites. At that time the Kenites were dwelling in the midst of the enemy, and Saul enjoined them to depart (1 Samuel 15:6), and in simple obedience they departed, so giving a lesson in obedience which Saul that day might well have taken to heart, and to have learnt before it was too late that to obey is better than sacrifice. We mention this incident because we believe that the simple character of the Kenites here revealed is manifested throughout their history, and as we have seen, from the events recorded in Jeremiah, their descendants the Rechabites also showed this same character.

The history of these particular Kenites begins, so far as our purposes are concerned, in Exodus 2, for we see from Judges 1:16 that the father-in-law of Moses was a Kenite. We note that this man Reuel was a priest of Midian (Exodus 2:16), and that Moses was "content to dwell with the man" (verse 21). We may get help as to this by noting that the name "Reuel" means "friend of God." We can only speculate as to how this man functioned as a priest, but his name must definitely indicate that he knew something of God. As a matter of fact, Genesis 25:2 shows that the Midianites were descended from Abraham through Keturah, after the death of Sarah, so it is not very strange that a man of this race should own the friendship of God. It is not strange, either, for Moses in the perplexity and fear of his heart to be content to dwell with a man of this character. It is a very great thing indeed to have realized that the friendship of God and with God is something worthwhile, though, alas, many make no further progress than this.

For the purposes we have in view it is needful to consider this man's history. We meet him again in Exodus 18, and we note that his name is now given as Jethro but in order that we shall not be led astray the Scriptures repeatedly call Jethro the father-in-law of Moses in this chapter. It is a graphic story. Jethro comes to the camp after the deliverance from Egypt a man of presence and power, for Moses "bowed down" (verse 7): and all the elders of Israel came to eat bread with him. The confession of Jethro in verse 11-15 is very interesting: "Now I know that the Lord is greater than all gods." There can be no doubt at all that Jethro had knowledge of Jehovah, and we must carefully note that he exercised this knowledge as he rendered a burnt-offering and sacrifices. The most remarkable thing to note, however, is that the elders of Israel came "to eat bread with Moses' father-in-law before God."

The scene next day is also of interest, when the advice of Jethro, manifestly sound, was accepted by Moses (verse 24). Alas, mere wisdom is not all, neither is knowledge, for the last verse of this chapter is to our mind one of the saddest in the Scriptures: "Then Moses let his father-in-law depart, and he went away to his own country." If it is permissible to speak, as we did as to Jehonadab's last will and testament, it is permissible to refer to this verse as the epitaph of Jethro. We read of him no more this wise and great man who in earlier days had been glad of the friendship of God, and "now knows" the Lord, and has seen the gathered people of God, yet does not cast in his lot with them. Maybe Moses did not ask him, for we read that Moses let him go.

The force of the expression just quoted is made all the greater when we consider the dealings of Moses with the son of this man, as recorded in Numbers 10:29-32. Moses pleads with Hobab, his brother-in-law: "We are setting out for the place of which the Lord said, 'I will give it you.' Come with us, and we will do good to you, for the Lord has promised good to Israel." Over a year has passed since the deliverance from Egypt (verse 11), and presumably Hobab has passed a considerable portion of his time with the people, he has seen the tabernacle and the provision of God for His service, and now has come the time of decision. He at least will not be allowed to go without receiving an invitation to stay.

We may well ask as to how it comes about that the father is allowed to go and the son is encouraged to stay. We believe that the key to it all is found in the meanings of the names of the two men. Reuel "friend of God," has become Jethro, which means "pre-eminent." Whether this eminence, dignity, or pre-eminence is due in some way to progress in his priestly office we know not, or whether that priestly office involves such a title we cannot say, but for our part we believe that in any case it expresses the changed character of the man, and if Exodus 18 is carefully read through again it will surely be apparent that there is indeed something dominating in the character of this man, as he receives obeisance, moves about the camp to criticise and advise, and speaks on equal terms with the men who have confronted kings on the behalf of Jehovah.

If it be true indeed that the name expresses the acquired character of the man then there can be no place for him among the people of God. One only can be pre-eminent, and if men seek pre-eminence they are in conflict with Christ (Colossians 1:18). In a later day Diotrophes merited lasting condemnation because he loved pre-eminence (3 John 9). It would have been ill for a people led by a man whose meekness was like that of the Master for whom he left the pleasures of Egypt, to have had to contend with the evil ensuing from a love of pre-eminence. So Moses "let him go."

It is true today that not many wise and not many noble are to be found among the people of God, but it is also true that while wisdom and nobility according to the estimation of this world might keep men from sharing with the people of God yet it is not the desire of God that people as such should be brought in to be a stumbling-block to the people. There is a wisdom which God values, but it comes from above and is associated with humility.

CHAPTER FOURTEEN: THE RECHAHITES (DR. A.T. DOODSON)

The difference in the actions of Moses with regard to Jethro and Hobab (Exodus 18; Numbers 10) is also explained by the meaning of Hobab, "beloved," and such as are beloved of God are desired by Him to be among His people. It should be noted also that Hobab is called the son of Reuel, and the reversion to the use of the earlier name of Jethro is emphasized by describing Reuel as the father-in-law of Moses, so that he should not be thought of as the son of Jethro. But some may ask, Are not Jethro and Reuel one and the same person? They are, but the changes in the usages of names should always be carefully noted. When God speaks of Jacob He refers to the same man as is also called Israel, but in different senses. Thus the tribe of Levi were to teach Jacob the judgements of God, and Israel the law of God. The former refers to Jacob and his descendants as men with all their natural weaknesses, while the latter name refers to the same people in covenant relation with God.

Thus Hobab is not called the son of Jethro but the son of Reuel. As the son bears something of the character of the father we therefore judge that in Hobab there was nothing of the love of pre-eminence which afflicted Jethro, but there was an appreciation of the friendship of God which had been the former glory of Reuel when Moses had been content to dwell with him. It is to such beloved ones that the call of God comes that they might be joined with the people of God. The call is clear and firm: "We are journeying to the place." If we are to pass on the call to others we must be as sure as Moses that the place is known and that the declarations of God are for good unto His people.

"Come with us, and we will do good to you." Such is what comes to the ears of Hobab, and his response is interesting. Hobab is standing at the parting of the ways, and cannot realize that the consummation of that promise is to be found long centuries after in the days of the Rechabites. Hobab hesitates: "I will not go: but I will depart to mine own land, and to my kindred." I do not think that God judges a man for hesitating when the call of God comes to him. Far better to weigh up the cost, and the decision made to abide by it, lest displeasure be caused to God by the man who turns back. Untold results hung upon that decision of Hobab, though he knew it not. Humanly speaking, well might he hesitate. His own land, that of the Kenites, is described for us by Balaam: "Enduring is your dwelling-place, and your nest is set in the rock" (Numbers 24:21). His own land and kindred! The human heart is stirred at the thought, and to many it is a hard saying of the Lord Jesus concerning them that follow Him. In a day when the wilderness was a place where every man's hand was against his fellow's, it was an incomparable blessing to have a strong dwelling place, set in the rock. What is offered against all this? Association with a people lately out of bondage in Egypt, weak and despised of the tribes around them, unused to the desert warfare and the desert life, the prey of the warring nations across their path to Canaan. Such is the one side. On the other there is the internal weakness which has been amply apparent, dissension and murmuring are rife among them, and their position as the chosen people is unmatched by the condition which should prevail among them.

Their choice is not unlike that of Moses himself, and we could imagine Hobab recalling the history of the man who so confidently spoke to him. He hesitates, and the call of God comes again to him: "Please do not leave us, for you know where we should camp in the wilderness, and you will serve as eyes for us. 32 And if you do go with us, whatever good the Lord will do to us, the same will we do to you." (Numbers 10:31-32). A purpose in the call is made apparent. It can be truly said that God has a purpose in every man and woman receiving the call, and it behoves us all to ascertain in due course, so far as we may, the work for which we have been called. The man was beloved, but in addition there was a need for him.

"So they set out from the mount of the Lord." These are the words which follow the call. History shows that Hobab responded to the call, and that he and his after him were always esteemed by the Israelites, as Saul's words show. But what of the esteem by God? We cannot doubt that Hobab in his lifetime received some of the good which had been promised to him, though he never arrived at that place which had been so confidently spoken of by Moses. The man who was the son of "Reuel" could always derive some comfort from the thought of God in the midst, but his true reward will be found in eternity.

Long centuries have passed to bring one of Hobab's descendants next to the king in Israel. Is this the consummation? No, for we see from 2 Kings 10 that Jehonadab does not stay the course, as men judge it. Though he does the work of judgement with Jehu, there is no mention of any reward for his services. Jehu gets his wages, which is a different matter; earthly position is assured to Jehu and his children after him for four generations, and who knows what might have been added had his response to the blessing of God been different? "But Jehu was not careful to walk in the law of the Lord." (verse 31)

There can be no doubt that the man Jehonadab whom we judged to have been in the counsels of Elisha would have had no pleasure in association with a king who displaced an Ahab only to walk in the ways of Jeroboam. Please read Jeremiah 35 again and consider the commands which Jehonadab gave to his people after his excursion into public affairs. The name of the man means "God is liberal," and yet he did not take advantage of the liberty he had. It would have been easy to take a "broadminded" or "liberal" view of things, and to do good by using his position in Israel. But this man, instructed in the things of God, assesses at their proper value the things he has witnessed in Israel and the things to be seen in Jehu. For him it was needful to remember the old paths, and the first ways of God. His forefather Hobab had taken the choice and had thrown in his lot with a pilgrim people. Better far to have neither lands nor houses than to forget God and to dishonour His Name.

"You shall live in tents all your days." It meant sacrifice to maintain this separated character, this pilgrim garb, but the men of old had been strangers in the world, the heirs of the promises had dwelt in tents and had made it manifest that they were seeking after a country and a city not of this world. Such a narrow-minded and unprogressive people, as some would regard them, could never have been called "Jehonadabites," but it was highly appropriate that they should be called after Rechab, for that name comes from a root used to describe a horse and its rider, two beings moving in unity, and such were the Rechabites.

Much has been made of the injunction not to drink wine, and there are many so-called Rechabites of this world who have taken heed to the commandment relative to the wine, but yet have drunk deeply of the spirit of the age, such as is spoken of in 2 Timothy 3:2. Disobedience is a characteristic of the last days, but above all else the true Rechabite must be such that, denying ungodliness and worldly lusts, he will live "self-controlled, upright, and godly lives in the present age, waiting for our blessed hope, the appearing of the glory of our great God and Savior Jesus Christ, who gave himself for us to redeem us from all lawlessness and to purify for himself a people for his own possession who are zealous for good works" (Titus 2:12-14). These, I repeat, are the true Rechabites.

In a day of gross disobedience it is the simple obedience of the Rechabites which is commended by God. The reward is very striking: "Jonadab the son of Rechab shall never lack a man to stand before me for ever." There is hardly a promise made to men which can stand above this. Only the highest and noblest of the servants of God and of the heavenly host are said to stand before God. Thus Gabriel could say: "I am Gabriel. I stand in the presence of God." So Jehonadab got his reward, though Jehu got wages. We can be in no doubt as to which is the greater man, and we may be sure that the will of God is to reward all that will value obedience, separation, unity, and soberness, as manifested by the Rechabites of a past day, and enjoined upon the true Rechabites of this day.

CHAPTER FIFTEEN: THE CHERETHITES AND THE PELETHITES (DR. A.T. DOODSON)

Among the peoples referred to as being associated with the Israelites, though not by nature children of Israel, there are none which more closely typify the saints of this dispensation than do the peoples associated with David and Solomon. It is common knowledge that David is a type of the Lord Jesus Christ, not only when he was waiting for the consummation of his anointing and patiently enduring the persecution by Saul, but also when he was constrained to flee before Absalom. Solomon stands as the complement to David, typifying the reigning of the Lord Jesus Christ when He comes in power and great glory, to dazzle the eyes of men with the riches of His glory.

It is very remarkable that we find a group of men associated with David and Solomon in the scenes which are most significantly typical of those things which have to do with the Lord. If we turn to 2 Samuel 15:18 we have prominently brought before us the Cherethites, the Pelethites, and the Gittites. Owing to the fact that there were 600 of these men, it has been readily assumed by some that these were the same 600 men as those who joined David in the Cave of Adullam and who afterwards followed him into the land of the Philistines (see 1 Samuel 22:2; 23:13; 25:13; 27:2) unto Achish, king of Gath. We note, however, that the Gittites at least were not Israelites, for Ittai "the Gittite" (2 Samuel 15:19) was "a foreigner," and also "an exile" with his own place to which he might return.

David entreated him so to return and to "take back" his brethren (verse 20). These, of course, will be the Gittites referred to in verse 18. David says of Ittai and his men that they came "only yesterday," though it states explicitly in verse 18 that they came after David from Gath. It is abundantly clear, therefore, that the 600 men of verse 18 included at least a number of aliens, and that this group of 600 men could not be identical with the Adullamites.

Further, the Cherethites themselves are referred to as being in the land of the Philistines, and they were raided by the Amalekites at the time when Ziklag, David's possession in Gath, was burnt (1 Samuel 30:14). See also Ezekiel 25:16. We must conclude therefore that the Cherethites, Pelethites, and Gittites were men of the Philistine race, and that for some reason they had cast in their lot with that of David. It behoves us to enquire as to their motives, and perhaps we can discern something common to them all in what Ittai and Achish say unto David. The noble reply of Ittai to David's injunction has rung through the centuries and will be to his glory and honour through all eternity: "As the Lord lives, and as my lord the king lives, wherever my lord the king shall be, whether far death or for life, there also will your servant be."

Like Ruth the Moabitess, he also could say in effect "Do not urge me to leave you or to return from following you. For where you go I will go, and where you lodge I will lodge. Your people shall be my people, and your God my God." Achish's testimony to David (1 Samuel 29.9) was that David bad been good in his sight, "as an angel of God."

We pass over the circumstances which had led David to seek refuge with Achish in the land of the enemies of Israel, and we overlook the obvious deceit practised by David, just as we must needs pass over many other blemishes in men who yet are set forth in measure as types of the One who alone was perfect. What is of moment is that clearly David had revealed traits which had endeared him to Achish and the Gittites, and it is not only that David had bloomed before them as the flower of manhood and the prince of warriors, but he had impressed upon Achish that spirituality which had caused Achish to revere him as an angel of God. David had undoubtedly opened up the mind of Ittai to the beauty of Jehovah, the great I AM, by whom Ittai could take oath, "As the Lord lives" The love of these men for David transcended the love of Jonathan, for it was for David's God also. Like Ruth in regard to Naomi, it was "your people ... and your God."

We judge, therefore, that it was out of pure love for David and the son of David that these 600 men followed David out of Gath when the day came for David to be brought to the kingdom. But their love was not of the kind which could fade with prosperity, for the day came when David crossed the brook Kidron, weeping as he went, cursed and reviled by men, rejected by the people, betrayed by those whom he had loved, a type indeed of that greater One who would cross the same brook on the way to Gethsemane. But there were men with David whose love was too deeply rooted to be affected by the cold wind of adversity, and in the days of his rejection they were a comfort to him.

We pass now to another scene. David's days are well-nigh over, and the appointed heir to glory must be hurriedly crowned because of the usurper (please read 1 Kings 1:5). Men's hearts have again been stolen, and all the king's sons, the captains of the host, the high priest (verse 25), and the men of Judah (verse 9), have ranked themselves behind Adonijah. The day is come for the revelation of Solomon as the appointed king. We read that those who had not been called to share in the festivities were "Nathan the prophet and Shimei and Rei and David's mighty men" (verse 8), also Zadok the priest, and Benaiah, and Solomon (verse 26). What action the mighty men took is not clear, but we read that Nathan, Zadok, and the mother of Solomon, bestirred themselves and brought the news to David, who commanded that Solomon should immediately be proclaimed as king.

The coronation of Solomon has some lessons for us, if we read aright. The men who took Solomon were "Zadok the priest, and Nathan the prophet, and Benaiah ... and the Cherethites and the Pelethites" (verse 38): that is, three Israelites and a band of aliens If it is correct, that these latter people were indeed gathered out of the land of the Philistines, and were thereby strangers to the covenants, we get a delightful picture of the great appearing in glory of our Lord Jesus Christ. When He comes on the clouds of heaven with power and great glory, who will be with Him? Not many mighty men, perhaps; very few Israelites, probably; but many who once had no hope, but were aliens and strangers, but will be then with Christ in glory. Once they were as the Philistines, proud men by nature (Zechariah 9:6), but their hearts were drawn after the Man of Sorrows, the One who was rejected and cast out by men, so that in their love for Him they humbled their hearts to love and serve and follow Him.

In that day of glory, He will be marvelled at, not only because of His intrinsic glory, but marvelled at in all them that believed; He will be glorified in His saints (2 Thessalonians 1:10). Men will be amazed to recognize in that train of the great King some whom they had esteemed as of no account upon the earth, men who had walked as pilgrims and strangers, having no part or lot in the things of the commonwealth of men, because their heart's love was set upon the Person of their great God and Saviour.

CHAPTER SIXTEEN: THE BONDSERVANTS OF SOLOMON (A.T. DOODSON)

The people who returned with Ezra and Nehemiah to the land of Israel were divided by them into five classes: "Israel, the priests, the Levites, the Nethinim, and the children of Solomon's servants" (Nehemiah 11:8, Ezra 2:43, 55, 58). We take it that the Nethinim are the descendants of those Gibeonites of whom we wrote in chapter twelve, who by their wiliness saved themselves from destruction at the hand of Joshua, and who were made to be hewers of wood and drawers of water for the sanctuary. It was shown in that chapter that these men, by the wisdom of God, were caused to be associated with the sanctuary, and consequently they were never, so far as we know, a snare to Israel, but occupied ultimately a place of honourable mention among a returned remnant.

We shall now seek to show that "the servants of Solomon" have a history which has a measure of similarity to that of the Gibeonites, and which provides striking lessons for us in that they were strangers to the covenants, yet partook in a real sense of the blessings of Israel. The servants of Solomon are without question the men referred to in connection with the building of the temple. It is well known that men who were not Israelites at all were employed by Solomon, and we may particularize Hiram, King of Tyre, and his servants. The builders were divided into three classes, Solomon's builders, Hiram's builders, and the Gebalites. It is not our intention to consider the last two classes for they received their wages for their services (1 Kings 9:11-18), though we note in passing that Hiram had a deeper reason than that of commercial prosperity, for he" was ever a lover of David" (1 Kings 5:1).

Solomon's builders appear to include three classes:

THE NATIONS OF THE OLD TESTAMENT

(1) "forced labor out of all Israel" (1 Kings 5:13) composed of 30,000 men in a rota of 10,000 men;

(2) 80,000 men that were hewers in the mountains, and 70,000 men that bore burdens (1 Kings 5:15);

(3) men drafted to be slaves (1 Kings 9:21), which did not include any man of Israel (verse 22).

In addition to these there were certain overseers that were probably Israelites. The first of these classes possibly were men of Israel, though there is a little doubt as to this in view of what is said in 1 Kings 9:15) which appears to refer to "the draft" as though there were only one, but we may pass over that point for the second and third classes included far more men. The second class were definitely strangers in Israel, gathered by David (1 Chronicles 22:2) and later by Solomon, men who perhaps were conscripted, but who otherwise had no permanent association with Israel. The third class was composed of the people that were left of the Amorites, the Hittites, the Perizzites, the Hivites, and the Jebusites, the descendants of the people whom the children of Israel would not, or could not, drive out from the land, for these men were determined to stay, and the congregation made them servants.

The Jebusites merit special mention. They were the original inhabitants of Jerusalem until David took the city and called it the city of David, and it was the threshing floor of a man of that race, Oman the Jebusite, where the angel of God chose to stand between the earth and the heaven, when David's sin of numbering the people caused God to send a pestilence (1 Chronicles 21:15), and there David was commanded to rear an altar to Jehovah.

It is passing strange that God should choose the house of a Jebusite, but it stirs one's heart to read the words of Oman after he had seen the angel of God (verses 20-25). There was a full surrender of a man's heart with an understanding of the things pertaining to the altar: the wood, the oxen, and the meal. There would seem to be a connection between this event and the act of Solomon when he took the Jebusites and their fellows, the Amorites, the Hittites and the rest, to make them builders of the Temple. At one time God had proclaimed everlasting enmity with men of these races. It had been His desire that they should be entirely driven out, but, because of the feebleness of the Israelites, and perhaps their desire for servants to set to taskwork (Joshua 16:10 and Judges 1:28), they had been allowed to stay in the land to provide snares for the people, until God in His anger deliberately left the residue of these Canaanites there that by them He might prove Israel (Judges 2:20-3:6). It was indeed a sad day for the Israelites when they took Canaanites to be their personal servants. A better example had been set them in connection with the Gibeonites, as was mentioned earlier, and the time had now come in the goodness of God when there was to be a reversion to that first example, and the Canaanites were levied from their places as servants of the people, to be servants to Solomon the glorious king, and to be brought into close relationship to the things of God in connection with His House.

It is not therefore now very surprising to find in a later day many of the descendants of these bondsmen in that ripe spiritual condition which led them to forsake the things of Babylon and to love the Place of the Name when very many Israelites were content to remain away from the Land and the Place. They were strangers indeed to the covenants and were not children of Abraham after the flesh, but truly children of Abraham according to faith, with a place of honour in the roll of the faithful remnant.

The ways of God are still the same, for men must be brought to understand the things of God, and caused to realize His holiness as well as His loving-kindness. Away from the House, men please themselves; in the House they are taught to obey; away from the House they may deem any kind of service to be sufficient, but in the House it must be strictly according to the revealed will of God. That will of God for the strangers to the covenants who are brought nigh today is expressed in the word of God. It is the Way of God for men today to be saved and also to be brought into (or planted in) the House of God. In this dispensation the number of Israelites in the House is very small, yet to such men as Paul was given the oversight of the building as committed to them by Him who builds the House.

As we ponder this story of the Canaanites who were determined not to be driven out, but who found an ultimate place in God's purposes, we might well bow ourselves before Him who foreknew us and caused us to be inheritors of the promises, though once we were far off and were strangers to the covenants. Well might we ponder, too, the fact that God's blessing to these strangers was only consummated when they were brought into close relationship to the things of the House of God.

Did you love *The Nations of the Old Testament: Their Relationship with Israel and Bible Prophecy*? Then you should read *Tribes and Tribulations - Israel's Predicted Personalities*[1] by Brian Johnston!

Naphtali, Manasseh, Gad, Asher...Of course, these are four of the tribes of Israel - you probably recognize their names but little more than that. Is there anything else to know about them? Bible teacher Brian Johnston answers that question with a resounding "yes" and points out that each of the original brothers had their own distinct characteristics and that, as prophesied, these traits would be replicated in their descendants. In addition, Brian also pinpoints a challenge for the reader from each tribe regarding their own character and relationship with God.

---

1. https://books2read.com/u/4NRlPJ

2. https://books2read.com/u/4NRlPJ

"Tribes and Tribulations" is an excellent addition to the popular "Search for Truth" Series.

1. Reuben: The Erring Brother
2. Simeon: The Wilful Brother
3. Levi: The Forceful Brother
4. Judah: The Leader Brother
5. Zebulun: The Single-Minded Brother
6. Issachar : The Serving Brother
7. Dan: The Ill-disciplined Brother
8. Naphtali: The Sharing Brother
9. Gad: The Overcoming Brother
10. Asher: The Quiet Brother
11. Manasseh & Ephraim: The Competitive Brother
12. Benjamin: The Courageous Brother

Also by Hayes Press

Bible Studies
Bible Studies 1990 - First Samuel
Bible Studies 1991 - The First Letter of Paul to the Corinthians
Bible Studies 1993 - Second Samuel
Bible Studies 1994 - The Establishment and Development of Churches of God
Bible Studies 1995 - The Kings of Judah and Israel from Solomon to Asa
Bible Studies 1992 - The Second Letter of Paul to the Corinthians

Needed Truth
Needed Truth 1888
Needed Truth 2001
Needed Truth 2002
Needed Truth 2003
Needed Truth 2004
Needed Truth 2005
Needed Truth 2006
Needed Truth 2007
Needed Truth 2008
Needed Truth 2009
Needed Truth 2010

Needed Truth 2011
Needed Truth 2012
Needed Truth 2015
Needed Truth 1888-1988: A Centenary Review of Major Themes

Standalone
The Road Through Calvary: 40 Devotional Readings
Lovers of God's House
Different Discipleship: Jesus' Sermon on the Mount
The House of God: Past, Present and Future
The Kingdom of God
Knowing God: His Names and Nature
Churches of God: Their Biblical Constitution and Functions
Four Books About Jesus
Collected Writings On ... Exploring Biblical Fellowship
Collected Writings On ... Exploring Biblical Hope
Collected Writings On ... The Cross of Christ
Builders for God
Collected Writings On ... Exploring Biblical Faithfulness
Collected Writings On ... Exploring Biblical Joy
Possessing the Land: Spiritual Lessons from Joshua
Collected Writings On ... Exploring Biblical Holiness
Collected Writings On ... Exploring Biblical Faith
Collected Writings On ... Exploring Biblical Love
These Three Remain...Exploring Biblical Faith, Hope and Love
The Teaching and Testimony of the Apostles
Pressure Points - Biblical Advice for 20 of Life's Biggest Challenges
More Than a Saviour: Exploring the Person and Work of Jesus
The Psalms: Volumes 1-4 Boxset
The Faith: Outlines of Scripture Doctrine
Key Doctrines of the Christian Gospel

Is There a Purpose to Life?
An Introduction to Bible Covenants
The Hidden Christ - Volume 2: Types and Shadows in Offerings and Sacrifices
The Hidden Christ Volume 1: Types and Shadows in the Old Testament
The Hidden Christ - Volume 3: Types and Shadows in Genesis
Heavenly Meanings - The Parables of Jesus
Fisherman to Follower: The Life and Teaching of Simon Peter
Called to Serve: Lessons from the Levites
Needed Truth 2017 Issue 1
The Breaking of the Bread: Its History, Its Observance, Its Meaning
Great Spiritual Revivals
An Introduction to the Book of Hebrews
The Holy Spirit and the Believer
Exploring The Psalms: Volume 1 - Thoughts on Key Themes
Exploring The Psalms: Volume 2 - Exploring Key Elements
Exploring the Psalms: Volume 3 - Surveying Key Sections
The Psalms: Volume 4 - Savouring Choice Selections
Profiles of the Prophets
The Hidden Christ - Volumes 1-4 Box Set
The Hidden Christ - Volume 4: Types and Shadows in Israel's Tabernacle
Baptism - Its Meaning and Teaching
Conflict and Controversy in the Church of God in Corinth
In the Shadow of Calvary: A Bible Study of John 12-17
Moses: God's Deliverer
Sparkling Facets: Bible Names and Titles of Jesus
A Little Book About Being Christlike
Keys to Church Growth
From Shepherd Boy to Sovereign: The Life of David
Back to Basics: A Study of Core Bible Teaching and Practice
An Introduction to the Holy Spirit

Israel and the Church in Bible Prophecy
"Growth and Fruit" and Other Writings by John Drain
15 Hot Topics For Today's Christian
Needed Truth Volume 2 1889
Studies on the Return of Christ
Studies on the Resurrection of Christ
Needed Truth Volume 3 1890
The Nations of the Old Testament: Their Relationship with Israel and Bible Prophecy
The Message of the Minor Prophets
Insights from Isaiah
The Bible - Its Inspiration and Authority
Lessons from Ezra and Nehemiah
A Bible Study of God's Names For His People
Moses in One Hour
Abundant Christianity
Prayer in the New Testament

About the Publisher

Hayes Press (www.hayespress.org) is a registered charity in the United Kingdom, whose primary mission is to disseminate the Word of God, mainly through literature. It is one of the largest distributors of gospel tracts and leaflets in the United Kingdom, with over 100 titles and hundreds of thousands despatched annually. In addition to paperbacks and eBooks, Hayes Press also publishes Plus Eagles Wings, a fun and educational Bible magazine for children, and Golden Bells, a popular daily Bible reading calendar in wall or desk formats. Also available are over 100 Bibles in many different versions, shapes and sizes, Bible text posters and much more!

www.ingramcontent.com/pod-product-compliance
Lightning Source LLC
Chambersburg PA
CBHW061335040426
42444CB00011B/2932